W9-AYF-308

God of

Many

Loves

God of

Many

Loves

Max Oliva, S.J.

ave maria press   Notre Dame, Indiana

© 2001 by Ave Maria Press, Inc.

International Standard Book Number: 0-87793-707-9

Cover and text design by Katherine Robinson Coleman

Printed and bound in the United States of America.

Library of Congress Cataloging-in-Publication Data
Oliva, Max.
God of many loves / Max Oliva.
      p. cm.
Includes bibliographical references.
ISBN 0-87793-707-9 (pbk.)
1. God--Love. I. Title.
 BT140 .O45 2001
231'.6--dc21   00-011584
                                 CIP

*I*n memory of Herb Ibarra, Dick Gossman, and George Bruns, who inspired me by their lives of faith and genuine goodness.

In memory of Kathy Ash, Craig Adams, Jim Sunderland, and Lorretta Doore ("Holy Feather"), my Canadian "angels" who watch over me in my new home.

To those who have taught me about the love of God, especially my parents and grandparents. In remembrance also of all my relatives, living and deceased, who passed on the Christian faith to me by word and example.

Contents

Acknowledgments

When the idea came to me to write this book on the love of God and its impact on our lives, it seemed only natural to engage others and their stories in the project. I especially want to thank the following friends, from Canada and the United States, who reflected on the questions listed at the end of the Introduction and shared their insights openly and profoundly. They are Pam Pawlak, Jack Hawkes, Laura Hiner, Terry Hiner, John Cotton, Margaret Powell, Larry Powell, Marge Price, Mary Ann Rossetti, Bev Pamenter, Mary Ann Shields, Denny Shields, Davey Williams, Geraldine Williams, Joyce Morey, and Terry Morey.

I am also grateful to Bob and Audrey Breaker, Clyde and Lavina Crossguns, Roy and Judy Copithorne, Bob and Nancy Jean Taylor, Ardyth and Gary Taylor, Amedo Cortese, and Al Campbell for their contributions.

Special thanks to Sister Eleanor Geever, C.C.V.I., for her friendship and encouragement; to Father Joe Conwell, S.J., for his long-term spiritual guidance, a relationship I deeply cherish; to Sister Mary Ann Fay, R.S.C.J., for the wisdom and gentle counsel over many years; and to Mary Robertson, Sister Celine Milette, S.P., and Fathers Burke Hoschka and Bill Stevenson for their support of my ministry in Alberta.

I wrote most of the book on the Siksika (Blackfoot) Reserve, in southern Alberta, Canada, and so I want to express my appreciation especially to the parishioners of Holy Trinity Mission who have been so welcoming and hospitable to me.

I owe my editor, Bob Hamma, distinct thanks. This is our third project together. I especially admire the gentle way he suggests changes in the text as well as the genuine interest he shows in an author's work.

And, most of all, I thank God, who has showered so much love on me, even before I was born.

Introduction

When I was a child, my image of God was that of a judge and the predominant emotion was fear. I was raised in the Roman Catholic church before the Second Vatican Council (1962-1965). My parents, the sisters who taught me religion, and I were brought up on the Baltimore Catechism. This book posed a number of questions about the existence of God that were answered in simple, easy to memorize words, questions like, "Who is God? God is the Supreme Being who created heaven and earth." There was nothing personal here, at least for me.

God as a judge meant frequent confession because one didn't want to get caught unprepared for a sudden death with sin on one's soul. Fear of hell and guilt motivated me as a child far more than desire for virtue or the goal of being a good person.

What was your image of God when you were a child? How did you relate to the Creator? Was it as loving father or mother, shepherd,

*lawgiver, liberator . . . ? What emotion best
describes how you felt about God?*

It wasn't until I was in my middle twenties that the
idea of God as caring and loving entered my
consciousness in a consistent way. This realization
was to have a profound effect not only on my faith life
but also on how I viewed myself. I grew up with a low
self-esteem, the result of a number of factors, one
being the fear that I was frequently letting God down
by sinful behavior. My confessions (weekly until I was
in my late teens) seemed so repetitive, the same sins
week after week. Would I ever improve? I wondered.

My image of God has changed radically over the
years. I still have a sense of awe when I think of the
majesty of God, as did all the significant figures in
both the Old and New Testaments, but in place of a
fear of retribution for my transgressions, I have an
overwhelming sense of God's unconditional love—
and mercy. My religious motivation now is a desire to
love God in return by being the kind of person God
wishes me to be. I have a much better appreciation of
myself, too, as God's love has become the very cornerstone of my identity.

*Has your image of God in any way affected
how you look at yourself, how you value
yourself, your self-esteem? If you are an adult,
can you see any correlation between your
image of God and your self-image?*

For the past seven years I have been asking retreatants
to reflect on their image of God and their image of
themselves. And, on how they have experienced the
love of God in their lives. They have shared how ben-
eficial their reflections have been in making them
more aware of God's immediate presence in their

lives. Single people have shared. Parents and grand-parents have considered just what images of God they are passing on to their children and grandchildren.

In addition, in preparation for this book, I asked seventeen Christian lay friends of mine to respond to nine questions about their relationship with God. The questions are listed at the end of this Introduction. I have included many of their stories in the book. Their thoughtful responses are both profound and practical, insightful and inspiring. You may wish to respond to these questions yourself, along with those in the text, as you read this book. Perhaps the use of a journal will be helpful.

Each chapter in the book explains and describes a way in which we experience the love of God over a lifetime. It has been my experience and others' that the way we encounter God changes depending on what is happening in our life. At one time we may be in dire need of God's mercy, at another, of God's power to heal. Sometimes we need to be reassured of God's providential love. When difficult times come, we depend on God to strengthen and protect us. Each experience comes from a God of many loves.

As a Jesuit, I have been deeply influenced by the spirituality of St. Ignatius of Loyola, our founder. One of the graces Ignatius received was the facility to find God in all things. This book is about learning to *find God's love in all things.* May this journey of discovery enrich your faith-life as it has mine.

A God of Many Loves

1. What was your image of God when you were a child? How did you relate to God, for example, as a father, mother, shepherd, Great Spirit, judge, lawgiver, etc.?

2. What is your image of God now? How do you relate to God now? Who for you speaks with God's voice? In whom do you see the face of God, feel God's touch, for example, a child, a close friend, an elder, someone famous, someone simple . . . ?

3. Has your image of God in any way affected how you look at yourself, your self-image, as loved, judged, or . . . ?

4. In his first letter, St. John writes, "We have come to know and to believe in the love God has for us" (1 John 4:16). Explain how you have come to know and to believe in God's love for you. Use personal examples from your life.

5. Are there any passages from the Bible that speak to you of the love of God? Feel free to either list the book, chapter, and verse, with an explanation of why the passage is meaningful to you, or simply refer to a story from the Bible. Do the same with other sources, for example, a novel, a poem, a song, a movie. . . .

6. Do you experience God's love as personal? Please explain in what way(s). Have you ever experienced the love of God for you in your dreams?

7. God speaks through the prophet Isaiah in 43:4, "You are precious in my eyes, and glorious . . . and I love you." How do you *feel* when you reflect on these words?

8. God loves us in many and varied ways—as merciful, healing, liberating, unconditional, empowering and strengthening, protecting, providing, to name a few. What words would you use to describe your experience of God's love and why? Feel free to use examples from your own life.

9. Is there anything else you would like to share about your relationship with God?

One

The Personal Love of God

The image of God in us is primarily
a potential to take in the love of God.[1]

PETER HANNAN, S.J.

Our life is a love story. Whether we are Christian or
Jewish, Hindu or Muslim, we believe there is a God
who has called us into existence out of love. Be this
God called Allah or Yahweh, Abba or Imma, we are in
an intimate relationship with our creator. Our awareness of this affiliation may be strong or it may be
weak. We may feel the intimacy the author of Psalm
139 did:

> [Lord] You created every part of me;
> you put me together in my mother's womb. . . .
> You saw me before I was born
> (Psalm 139:13, 15).

Or, our image of God may be so distant and theo-
retical that our appreciation of God's presence in our
life is minimal. I recall the story of a married man who
was on a retreat. He was earnestly seeking to know
God in his heart and not just in his head. His retreat
director suggested he imagine God holding him in his

arms. Try as he did the retreatant could not get the image. He was about to give up when the memory of his wife's hands came to him, hands that had lovingly caressed him for so many years. Suddenly, he was overcome with joy as he realized God's deep love for him through the tender love of his wife.

For many of us our image of God changes over the years. As children we can see God as benevolent or as harsh. Terry, a married man in his early fifties, recalls, "As a child God played the 'judge.' He had a white beard and soft gentle eyes. There was a degree of fear of this great judge even when my sins seemed small." Geraldine, who grew up in Northern Ireland in the 1950s, expresses a similar experience: "The God of my childhood was a vengeful God, ever vigilant of my childhood transgressions."

Penny, who was raised in western Canada, and is the mother of four children, shares, "My vision of God was distant when I was a child. I felt that God was strict, demanding, not very fair, and certainly did not want me to be joyful."

Contrast these accounts with the following three experiences. Pam was born and raised in England. She remembers: "My image of God as a child was of an old man with a white beard and white hair, sitting in a large chair holding out his arms to me. He looked just like my grandfather who I loved very much." Larry has a similar grandparent memory: "I felt I could talk to God as I talked with my grandfather, but the only time I felt God might speak to me was at night, when I was in bed, before I went to sleep. Then, I would ask him for help in school and at home." "My very first recollection of God came during a horrible thunderstorm in the middle of the night when I was four years old," recalls Mary Ann. "I was very frightened. My father came into my room, sat on the bed next to me and said, 'Don't be afraid, Mary Ann, that is just God and some of his friends bowling up in heaven! Listen for God's bowling ball to hit the pins, then watch for the lightening, which will tell you that he got a strike!' At that point in my relationship with God, I saw him as a happy, playful person with very bad timing!"

Peter Hannan writes, "The image of God in us is primarily a potential to take in the love of God."[2] Christians believe that the fundamental nature of God is Love: "God is love, and whoever lives in love lives in union with God and God lives in union with him/her" (1 John 4:16). Love is what constitutes God. In the Book of Genesis, we read: "Then God said: Let us make [human beings] in our image, after our likeness." "God created [human beings] in his image; in the divine image he created [them]" (1:26a, 27 NAB).

In other words, God has created us in such a way that we, too, can become love in as much as we are able to accept in the depths of our heart and spirit the love of God. This means, of course, embracing the God of suffering in our trials as well as the God of joy in our pleasant times. Perhaps the fullness of this love will not be ours until we are united with God after we die, but our lifelong journey can be a steady and ever deeper realization of this love.

We can deny that this love exists. We can turn away from it by choosing to follow other gods. We can lose sight of it through the circumstances of life—poverty, injustice, or an addiction. People may try to beat it out of us through putdowns or rejection. But, and this is key: *the potential to receive will not die.* All it needs is a little nourishment, a spark of love from someone else, a grace of insight, and the seed will grow, like what happened to the man who discovered God's love through the image of his wife's hands.

Like many others, my story involves finding the love of God in my life gradually. Since my image of

God as a child was of a judge, my primary emotion the fear of hell, God as love was not uppermost in my mind. Until something quite out of the ordinary happened. I was a junior in college, about nineteen years old. At the time, I was dating a wonderful girl, and we had recently expressed our love for one another. A few days after this declaration of our love, the following message came into my consciousness, "No one can ever love you as much as I do." I knew without a doubt that this was God speaking. To my recollection this was the first *personal* encounter I had with God. I wasn't to appreciate the full extent of this revelation until five years later when I realized I had a vocation to be a priest.

Are you able to recall a moment, an event, an experience that changed your perception of God, at whatever age?

Joyce remembers the first time she knew for certain that there is a God and that he loves and cares for her:

> I was about thirteen and, although for the most part my life was good, I had one really big problem. I was very, very much afraid of the dark! I was also blessed with an active imagination. I grew up in Scotland and in those days there was no such thing as a built-in closet. In my bedroom I had this huge wooden wardrobe. This, of course, was where my imaginary intruder/attacker was hiding. So, every night I would go to bed afraid to fall asleep lest this would be the night when he would come and get me. In my fear, one night, I called out to my heavenly Father. Suddenly there came over me such a feeling of peace. It seemed to fill up my whole room. The presence of this peace

was so physical that I reached my arm from beneath the bedcovers to touch it and I said into the darkness, "Hello, God."

Sometimes this awareness of God's personal love comes later in life. Geraldine recalls a significant incident when her experience of God changed completely:

I first came to believe in God's love for me the day he delivered my eight-year-old daughter, Julie, from the grip of death. Her trachea had swollen virtually closed during a bout with croup. I was holding her in my arms as we sat on our doorstep waiting for the ambulance to arrive. I looked up at the frigid December sky and fervently prayed that my beloved child, lifeless and blue, would be returned to me healthy. The expertise of the paramedics and the staff in the intensive care unit of the hospital combined to successfully resuscitate my daughter and restored her to perfect health. For me, it was a miracle.

Davey is an adult convert to Catholicism. All was not smooth in the transition, as he shares:

For many years after my conversion, I had a difficult time accepting communion in the meaning of the Catholic church, as the real body and blood of Christ. One morning, after working the night shift, I came home and went to bed. There had been nothing special about the day that had me thinking about my faith; it was just another day. I fell asleep quickly and slept soundly. In a dream, I found myself in a church. It was pure white with everything having a marble-like texture. I was standing in what I can only describe as the choir balcony. I looked down and across the interior of the church and saw Our Lady. She beckoned me to come down to the lower level, which I did. I came to a large crucifix on the wall and looked up at it. As I did so, Christ's arms came away from the cross and his hands came together. As he opened his hands, a round disk fell from them. It seemed to fall very slowly, turning round and round as it descended. I put out my hands to catch the disk, and when I did I saw it was a communion wafer. I placed it in my mouth. "This *is* my Body," was clearly the message. I awoke with a start at that point, sweating and fearful, fully expecting God to be in the room. Of course, he wasn't, but since that night I have not missed receiving communion.

The image of God in us can be blurred by low self-esteem. Consider the following fable and the lesson we can draw from it.

There was a little girl called Rapunzel who was very beautiful. She was captured by a witch, who knew that if she wanted to hold onto the little girl, she had to convince her that she was ugly. If she knew she was beautiful, she would go off with one of the many young men who came to consult the witch. If, on the other hand, she knew she was ugly, she would be afraid of being seen by them, and would therefore hide when they were around. So the witch gradually convinced Rapunzel that she was ugly, and she hid for fear of being seen when anyone came to the witch's house. One day when she was combing her hair in her room, she became conscious of someone looking at her through the window. Instinctively she looked up. It was then that she saw, in the eyes of the young man gazing at her through the window, that she was beautiful. Gradually, as she learned to believe this, her fear was replaced by joy. She set off on the long journey of freeing herself from the deadening influence of the witch in order to accept the life and happiness which the young man's love made available to her.[3]

What is highlighted in this story are the two images we can have of ourselves, one true, one false. And there are two voices: one from without that tells us we are not smart enough, not good looking enough, not popular enough, not successful enough, the other from within telling us, in the words of the prophet Isaiah, "you are precious in my eyes and glorious, and . . . I love you" (43:4 NAB). Which voice do we listen to most?

In the parable of the sower and the seed, Jesus gives us a lesson on cultivating good soil, that is, a heart open to receiving the good news. And, what is the good news? It is that we are loved by a God whose very essence is love.

Once there was a man who went out to sow grain. As he scattered the seed in the field, some of it fell along the path, and the birds came and ate it up. Some of it fell on rocky ground, where there was little soil. The seeds soon sprouted, because the soil wasn't deep. But when the sun came up, it burned the young plants; and because the roots had not grown deep enough, the plants soon dried up. Some of the seed fell among thorn bushes, which grew up and choked the plants. But some seed fell in good soil, and the plants bore grain: some had one hundred grains, others sixty, and others thirty (Matthew 13:3-8).

What does this parable have to say to us on the theme of God's love and our heart?

The path is often walked on, the earth is hard, not receptive to the seed. Perhaps we too have been "walked on" by putdowns or some form of rejection from others. We have listened because our self-image is low. Rocky ground has some soil, but not enough for the seed to take root; we may have some self-appreciation but not enough to withstand a trial, a cross, a difficulty in life. Thorn bushes choke the plants; they are like the guilt we feel for past mistakes, or the inability to forgive ourselves for some wrong, and the feeling that we have to *earn* God's love by doing good deeds. When we don't think we need God because of our pride, our identity is wrapped up in what we have instead of who we are, a personal tragedy leads us to mistrust God, and so forth. These are "thorns of the heart" that need to be cleared so that the good soil within can fully receive the love God wishes to give.

We may need spiritual open-heart surgery!

After my experience of knowing of God's love for me at the age of nineteen, I continued my journey, eventually finishing college. I traveled in Europe for four months, served in the United States Coast Guard in a special reserve program for college graduates, worked as a salesman for a food cannery, and lived a normal social life.[4] Until one day, while in my office at the cannery, when a completely unexpected idea came to me, "I think I want to be a priest." This thought completely stunned me. However, it was as clear in my consciousness as the revelation of God's love had been five years before. One month later I entered the Jesuit novitiate.

It was in the novitiate that my awareness of a personal God who was interested in me came to light again, and this time, deepened. Alone, without my possessions to shore up my identity, I realized my self-image was shaky. I see now, I was a vessel waiting to be filled. Through the help of an inspired spiritual advisor, I began meditating on Bible texts that stressed God's love. He encouraged me to read the passages as if God was addressing me personally.

One of my favorite passages, then and now, is from the prophet Isaiah. Here is how I learned to pray it:

> But now, thus says the Lord,
> who created me and formed me;
> Fear not, for I have redeemed you;
> I have called you by name: you are mine. . . .
> You are precious in my eyes
> and glorious, and I love you
>   (Isaiah 43:1, 4 NAB adapted).

I spent hours reflecting on this text, soaking it up like a sponge.

At first, it was an intellectual exercise. Then one day, I just knew in the depths of my being the truth of God's love for me. Thanks to the ongoing grace of God I still stand on this spiritual cornerstone today.

Years later, I came across the poetry of Rabindranath Tagore. The following poem eloquently describes my journey as well as his:

> Thou hast made me endless, such is thy pleasure.
> This frail vessel thou emptiest again and again,
> and fillest it ever with fresh life.
>
> This little flute of a reed thou hast carried
> over hills and dales,

and hast breathed through it melodies eternally
new.

At the immortal touch of thy hands
my little heart loses its limits in joy
and gives birth to utterance ineffable.

Thy infinite gifts come to me only
on these very small hands of mine. Ages pass
and still thou pourest,
and still there is room to fill.[5]

*How have you come to know and to believe
in God's love for you? Was it through the love
of another? Did it come through the birth of
your first child? Were you contemplating a
sunset or leisurely fishing a mountain stream?
Did God speak to your heart through a passage in the Bible or an exquisite poem? Where
do you see the face of God?*

Jack, now retired, recalls his early experience of God
as One who punishes us for our mistakes. Through
some difficult struggles, he has learned to have complete faith in a forgiving God rather than a vengeful
one, one he can turn to for guidance and strength.

Kathy, who grew up in a strict family and saw
God as a judge in her childhood, now finds the love of
God for her at the end of each Mass she attends:
"When the priest gives the final blessing, I imagine
God placing his hand on my head and I am at peace."

Susan is a member of her parish choir. She shares
how she came to the realization of God's love for her:
"I hear the voice of God in music, all kinds of music,
sacred and otherwise. I can be moved to tears of
gratitude by some musical piece. I relate to God as a

source of great comfort, being wrapped in his mantle or being in the shelter of his wings."

Some of us find the love of God in our marriage partner. As John, who has been married for forty years, relates, "I see the face of God fleetingly in many people, but especially and most often in my wife." Mary Ann, who is recently married at the age of forty-two, shares her experience:

> It was not until after Denny and I were married that I finally realized the extent of God's love for me. I have always thought that friends liked me and my parents loved me, but through the sacrament of marriage, I have become vividly aware that Denny's love for me is *never* ending, that he would do anything for me. Incredibly, to me, I feel that I am now able to see the face of God in my husband. As I rest next to him, or look over the dining room table at him, or watch him sleep, I see God's face; I see and know that God exists prominently in Denny for me.

Father, Son, Holy Spirit

The person of the Trinity to whom we pray and relate as the one who loves us may change as we grow older. I did not have a good relationship with my father until I was in my late twenties. Likewise, I did not pray to God as Father until my dad and I began being friends. My sense of God when I joined the Jesuits was beyond gender. Early in the Jesuit novitiate, I meditated on what St. Ignatius called the "Principle and Foundation" of one's life. The first part of the reflection is: "The goal of our life is to live with God forever. God gave us life because God loves us. Our own response of love allows God's life to flow

into us without limit."[6] I related to God as creator and
as the one who had miraculously entered my life and
invited me to be his servant. Before I joined the
Jesuits, there was a lack of meaning in my life. In the
novitiate, I found it.

Now, as I look back over the past thirty-seven
years of Jesuit life, I see how I have related to God as
Father in a variety of ways. Just making the sign of the
cross puts me in mind of God's paternity. In celebrating Mass, the Father is often mentioned, especially in
eucharistic prayers three and four. Jesus taught us to
call God "Abba," which is as endearing a term as
papa or daddy. The intimacy of calling God "Abba,"
has deepened our relationship. "Nothing [is] impossible with God" (Luke 1:37 NAB) is an encouraging
message that has often appeared in my consciousness
as I have been called to do something I thought
beyond my capability. Occasionally, I have heard the
words in my heart, "you are my son in whom I am
well pleased." Other people, men and women, have
told me they have had this affirmation as well. In the
next chapter we will consider yet another aspect of
God as loving father when we reflect on the parable of
the prodigal son. And, as we begin the third millennium, wondering perhaps at times if this is the end
time, Jesus reminds us that only the Father knows
when that will happen. We are to simply trust in him.

I have met people who also had a bad father experience, but unlike my story they found the father they
were looking for in God before they were reconciled
with their earthly parent.

It was in my early days as a Jesuit that I discovered
Jesus as a person I could relate to and pray to. My
awakening came through a form of prayer where you
use your imagination. In this prayer you choose a
passage from one of the gospels and imagine yourself
in the scene. In other words, you are there when Jesus

heals the man with leprosy or the woman with a hemorrhage; you are in the boat with Peter and the other apostles when Jesus comes walking on the water; you are at the Last Supper when Jesus washes the feet of those present. The purpose of this method of prayer is to get to know Jesus more intimately, to fall in love, or more in love, with him by getting to know his personality, his values, his mind and heart. You can even become one of the characters in the scene and experience Jesus' healing touch, loving gaze, soothing embrace.

This form of prayer was one of St. Ignatius' favorites. It is also known as "application of the senses" because you want to engage as much as possible your senses of seeing, listening, smelling, tasting, touching. What senses you use depends on the passage you choose. If you have a good imagination, which I discovered I have, this can be a powerful way to realize your friendship with the Lord.

Through the prayer of the imagination, Jesus took on human form for me. We became friends. I got to know better not only him but myself as well. He became my companion, my source of strength. There will be opportunities later on in the book to try this kind of prayer.

I think Pope John Paul II was inspired when he proclaimed the Jubilee to commemorate the beginning of the new millennium. At the heart of Jubilee is the call of God the Father to set people free and to do so out of love. "Love one another as I have loved you," Jesus told his disciples (John 15:12 NAB). "As the Father has loved me, so I have loved you" (15:9 NAB).

The first of three years of preparation for Jubilee 2000 focused on the person of Jesus, our brother and friend; the second, on our moral guide the Holy Spirit; and the third on God the Father, the One who created us, whose love keeps us in existence. Jubilee is a time for rejoicing but it is also a time for conversion, a turning away from any accommodation we have given to "false gods" and false images of God. It is a time to recall one of our most basic experiences of the God we believe in, as told to us in the Old Testament:

> When Israel was a child, I loved him
> and called him out of Egypt as my [child].
> But the more I called to him,
> the more he turned away from me.
> My people sacrificed to Baal;
> they burned incense to idols.
> Yet I was the one who taught Israel to walk.
> I took my people up in my arms,
> but they did not acknowledge that I took care of
>   them.
> I drew them to me with affection and love.
> I picked them up and held them to my cheek;
> I bent down to them and fed them
>   (Hosea 11:1-4).

This is each person's story: redemption, conversion, redemption.

The Holy Spirit plays a significant role in our faith history. There has been a resurgence of interest in the Spirit during the past forty years, due, in large part, to the charismatic renewal. Life in the Spirit seminars and parish prayer groups have attracted many people and given them a new way to pray. Speaking in tongues (a form of contemplative prayer), prayers for various kinds of healing, and reflection on the scriptures have brought many closer to God, some even back to the faith.

In his last discourse, Jesus told his disciples, "The Helper, the Holy Spirit, whom the Father will send in my name, will teach you everything and make you remember all that I told you" (John 14:26).

The Spirit is a sanctifying presence in the church and in the world. We need the seven gifts of the Spirit for our faith journey:

▸ *Wisdom* helps us to know what is truly pleasing to God and aids us in discerning what God wishes of us.

▸ *Understanding* leads us to truth and to compassion, it enables us to see life through the eyes of the other.

▸ *Courage* guides us safely through moments of suffering and death; it helps us to face our crosses with patient endurance and empowers us to face and succeed in the challenges that face us.

▸ *Knowledge* plunges us into the depth of God's love and mercy and helps us to show mercy to others; it encompasses both the mind and the heart, the whole person.

▸ *Right Judgment*, akin to wisdom, helps us to make the right moral choices in whatever situation we find ourselves.

▸ *Piety* aids us as we strive to live out the values of the gospel. It helps us to keep our faith alive in the midst of all the world's temptations, especially through prayer and the sacraments, and assists our efforts to grow in friendship with God.

▸ *Wonder and Awe in God's Presence*, traditionally known as "fear of the Lord," is a reverential attitude in the face of the mystery that is God. Knowing that no human being has all the answers gives us hope as we face the future, that God is in charge and good will triumph over evil.

We can, of course, ask the Spirit for an increase in these gifts as the occasion arises. Reflecting on the new millennium and the need for effective witnesses of the gospel, Bishop Robert F. Morneau wrote: "Through the work of the Holy Spirit and our cooperation, we put on the mind and heart of Jesus so that his wisdom and affection might touch the people and events of our day. The Spirit calls us and helps us to grow; the Spirit makes possible our bearing abundant fruit, fruit that lasts."[7]

In his book *Impelling Spirit,* Fr. Joseph Conwell describes the Holy Spirit as passionate, creative, innovative, wildly beyond the rational, propelling, driving, pushing, blowing like an untamed hurricane with no predictable path.[8] Both Mary and Joseph had experiences of this "wildly beyond the rational" in the conception of Jesus. We might say that they met the God of the unexpected. The Spirit can take us too in unexpected directions.

> Looking back over your life, are you able to see the effects of the Spirit in the decisions and directions your life has taken?
>
> How has the Spirit been a sanctifying presence in your journey?
>
> What gifts of the Spirit do you feel you need to pray for now?

Allow me to share an experience of being impelled by the Spirit in a very personal way. Impelled does not mean being deprived of your freedom. As Fr. Conwell explains, the power of the Holy Spirit does not take away our freedom but enhances it.

In the fall of 1995, I began giving parish missions and retreats in southern Alberta, Canada. I had never had any ministry in Canada before. I was very impressed by the number of people who came to the first mission, which was in the city of Calgary, the pastor really had promoted it. At the second mission, in a semi-rural area to the west of Calgary, I was totally taken with the faith and interest of both the pastor and the people in what I had to offer. I was invited to return to the diocese for Lent of 1996 and again was overwhelmed by both the turnout and the faith of the people. Thus began a series of trips from San Diego, California, where I lived at the time, to the Calgary diocese. I wasn't there all the time, but I was going up two, sometimes three, times a year for the next four years.

When I had a free weekend while in the diocese, I would help at an aboriginal, Blackfoot parish, located on a reserve (reservation) in the middle of the prairies. I knew I was being led by the Spirit—I even drove up twice! In the summer of 1998, I filled in for two pastors while they took their vacations. I spent the first part of this time at the Blackfoot mission. It was there that the seed of an idea began to form, one that came to fruition later during my annual retreat. I made the retreat shortly after I returned to San Diego after my summer work. The invitation, in my prayer, was clear: to ask my Provincial for permission to live and work in the Calgary diocese for two years, and to make the Blackfoot mission my base. The idea to do the latter had come from those who work at the mission.

"Creative" and "innovative" certainly describe the suggestion to do this for a number of reasons. First, there are no other Jesuits working in southern Alberta, hence no Jesuit community. This would be the first time I would have lived at a distance from other Jesuits, who I experience as my family. Second, I would be living on my own which I had only done for short periods before. And, third, the winter weather. I was going from the tropical climate of San Diego to the snow and ice of the north. While I was on retreat I asked God for the courage and the generosity to make the move. The Holy Spirit heard me: I began this book in San Diego, I finished it on the reserve.

The Feminine Face of God

When I look back on my life and the ways I have related to God, I am amazed that it wasn't until I was in my fifties that I thought about the feminine attributes of God. Amazed because, although I was at odds with my father until I was twenty-nine, my mother and I were best of friends. This was especially true when I was in my teens. Sadly, my mother died when I was twenty, leaving a big hole in my heart. However, her mother and I were also close, and she lived for seven years after my mother died.

Of course, God is beyond what we understand as person: father or mother. Jesus refers to God as father because we human beings are relational and we need to relate to the divine in terms of personhood. And, the times in which he lived were patriarchical. Mysticism can take us into the heart of God where we lose a sense of the relational, but most of the time we direct our prayers to Father, Son, or Holy Spirit. Or, as the Irish say, through the "back door," through Mary, if we are too timid to go direct! I came to the realization that God has both what we would call feminine and masculine traits by a different kind of back door.

I have been influenced by the psychology of Carl Jung who learned that each person is composed of both anima (feminine) and animus (masculine) elements. He wrote, "The anima is the female element in the male unconscious and the animus is the male element in the female unconscious."[9] A key task of the human journey is the integration of the two. My reasoning, then, took me in this direction: if human beings are made in the image and likeness of God, then God must also have both anima and animus in the Divine essence.

The Old Testament writers employed both father and mother images when describing the love of God. Speaking of the covenant relationship between God and the Israelites, Jeremiah wrote of a father: "Israel, you are my dearest son, the child I love best. Whenever I mention your name, I think of you with love. My heart goes out to you; I will be merciful" (31:20). This, after Israel had turned away from the covenant. In the following passage, when the people began to doubt God's limitless love, God spoke through the prophet Isaiah: "Can a woman forget her own baby and not love the child she bore? Even if a mother should forget her child, I will never forget you" (49:15).

Julian of Norwich, a mystic who lived in England in the late fourteenth century, received sixteen revelations of God's love. She experienced God as "our mother." Here are some excerpts:

> And so in our making, God almighty is our loving Father, and God all wisdom is our loving Mother, with the love and goodness of the Holy Spirit, which is all one God, one Lord. . . . I contemplated the work of all the Blessed Trinity, in which contemplation I saw and understood these three properties: the property of the fatherhood, and the property of the motherhood, and the property of the lordship in one God.

Interestingly, Julian often related to Jesus as mother:

> In the second person [of the Trinity], in knowledge and wisdom we have our perfection, as regards our sensuality, our

restoration and our salvation, for he is our
Mother, brother and saviour.

So Jesus Christ, who opposes good to evil, is
our true Mother.[10]

In recent times, some people have begun to pray
to the Holy Spirit using the pronoun "she," linking
the feminine description of wisdom (see Wisdom 6:12,
7:25-26; Sirach 14:20-27; and Proverbs 9) to the Spirit
who is the source of wisdom.

The more rational our way of thinking, the more
we might find feminine images of God difficult to
relate to. Bede Griffiths, a Benedictine monk who was
born in England and lived for many years in India,
struggled for most of his life to integrate the masculine and feminine—rational and intuitive—ways of
thinking and praying. His breakthrough finally came
at age eighty-four. He explains what happened one
morning at the Christian Ashram where he lived:

I had some breakfast and then I felt sort of
restless, disturbed, not knowing quite what
was happening. The inspiration came suddenly again to surrender to the Mother. It
was quite unexpected: "Surrender to the
Mother." And so I somehow made a surrender to the Mother. Then I had an experience
of overwhelming love. Waves of love sort of
flowed into me. . . . I called out, "I'm being
overwhelmed by love." At first I thought I
would die and just be engulfed in this love. It
was the "unconditional love" of which I had
often spoken, utterly mysterious, beyond
words.[11]

In being able to surrender to the feminine within
himself, Dom Bede had found the feminine in God.
He was taken to realms of darkness, to the depths of

the mystery of God. Later, he reflected: "God is not simply in the light, in the intelligible world, in the rational order. God is in the darkness, in the womb, in the Mother, in the chaos from which the order comes."[12]

All this goes to say that we need not feel limited in how we relate to God and God's love. Sometimes I pray to God as Father, at other times I meditate on a gospel passage in order to be with Jesus in my imagination, while at other times I am conscious of the power of the Holy Spirit in my life. Sometimes I experience the gentle love of God, as coming from a mother, at other times I am aware of the protective, fatherly love of God.

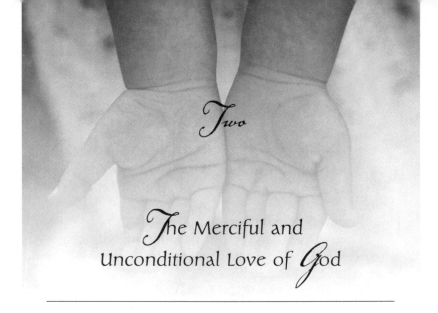

Two

The Merciful and Unconditional Love of God

Inside your temple, O God,
we think of your constant love.

PSALM 48:9

Has God found a home in me?

The Father knocks at my door, seeking a home for his Son.

"Rent is cheap," I say.

"I don't want to rent. I want to buy," says God.

"I'm not sure I want to sell, but you might come in to look around."

"I think I will," says God.

"I might let you have a room or two."

"I like it," says God. "I'll take the two. You might decide to give me more some day. I can wait."

"I'd like to give you more, God, but it's a bit difficult. I need some space for me."

"I know, but I'll wait. I like what I see."

"Hmmm, maybe I can let you have another room. I really don't need that much."

37

"Thanks. I'll take it. I like what I see."

"I'd like to give you the whole house . . . but I'm not sure."

"Think on it," says God. "I wouldn't put you out. Your house would be mine, and my Son would live in it. You'd have more space than you've ever had before."

"I don't understand at all."

"I know, but I can't tell you about that. You'll have to discover it for yourself. That can only happen if you let me have the whole house."

"A bit risky," I say.

"Yes," says God, "but try me."

"I'm not sure—I'll let you know."

"I can wait," says God. . . . "I like what I see."[1]

Does this dialogue sound familiar? Have you had a similar encounter with the unconditional love of God?

This is a God who not only gives love without conditions but also wants us to return the same kind of love to:

> Return to the Lord your God people of Israel . . . return to the Lord, and let this prayer be your offering to him: Forgive all our sins and accept our prayer, and we will praise you as we have promised (Hosea 14:1-2).

This is a God of merciful love!

Perhaps the story in the New Testament that most clearly speaks of both God's merciful and unconditional love is the parable of the Prodigal Son (Luke 15:11-32). Some writers on Christian spirituality have rightly pointed out that this story could be re-named "the prodigal father," for he is extravagant in his love for his wayward son. Unlike some fathers who would write a willful child out of their will, or at the least

ban the daughter or son from the family home for
some serious transgression, the prodigal father forgives everything and even throws a party to celebrate
his son's return. It doesn't take much of a stretch to
find contemporary parallels: a daughter who is preg-
nant and unmarried; a son who parties his way to
flunking out of college.

What is remarkable in the father's behavior in the
parable? Roland Faley suggests a number of things:

> The son's prepared speech is abbreviated in
> its actual recitation; no suggestion of a
> degraded status is allowed to be uttered. The
> reunion itself is poignantly dramatic. Even
> though running violates the norms of patri-
> archal propriety, the father does not hesitate
> to do so in his excitement at the son's return.
> The embrace and kiss take place with no
> questions asked. The son's total restoration
> to his place in the family is seen in the cere-
> monial robe, the signet ring, and sandals.
> The festive banquet lifts the occasion to an
> even higher level of acceptance.[2]

Can we rise to this level of unconditional love?
Three mothers share their experience.

Penny, parent of four teenagers, says:

> I think parenting has given me a way to
> understand unconditional love. Being a
> mother has helped me to understand the
> kind of love where giving my life for anoth-
> er is not much of a stretch. My children know
> that I love them, but I want them to under-
> stand what makes each an individual and
> precious to me because of the separate gifts
> God has given to each. As each one leaves
> home, I write them a letter telling them
> specifically why I love them. I end each letter

by telling them to remember how much I
love them, especially when they least love
themselves. This is how I understand God's
love and belief in me.

"The Biblical passage that most clearly speaks of
God's love for me is Isaiah 43:4: 'You are precious in
my eyes and glorious and . . . I love you,'" relates
Geraldine. "These words make me feel humble and
unworthy, but when I reflect on them I realize they are
the sentiments of a parent. I express similar feelings to
my children regardless of their acts and deeds."

"I feel God looks at me the way I look at my children." Joyce shares:

> Sure, sometimes they let me down, but most
> often when I am with them my heart is
> singing from sheer love for them. Sometimes
> my heart feels as though it will burst with
> this love and the pride I feel just in their exis-
> tence. I love my children not because they
> have become Nobel Peace Prize winners,
> (they haven't,) but because they just are. This
> is how I believe God loves me.

There is another key figure in the parable, the
elder son. He is appalled by the behavior of his father
as, no doubt, he was of his brother's chosen lifestyle.
It takes a determined effort by his father to show him
why celebration is in order: "Your brother was dead,
but now he is alive; he was lost, but now he has been
found" (Luke 15:32). Joy, not jealousy, is called for.

I have a friend, whose name is Denny, for whom
the elder son in the parable fits quite well. He told me
he always felt sympathy for the good son, having
been an obedient, faithful, dedicated, and loyal child
to his parents. This was the case until one day God
opened his eyes. He felt simultaneously humbled,

embarrassed, and tearful at this awakening to the extent of God's indiscriminate love.

In his poem "As It Is," Michael Suarez sums up what our attitude should be regarding who God loves and why.

1.

The giver is the gift
Again the gift is present, undiminished.

The giver is without limits,
love universal, but specific,

prizing everything precious,
as it is.

2.
Disbuild the tower you have raised
scatter the treasure you have saved

forget the points you'd thought you'd earned
for good behavior.

The giver is the gift of worth:
you do not get what you deserve.[3]

Victor Hugo wrote, "The supreme happiness in life is the conviction of being loved." Certainly, this has been my experience. As I mentioned in Chapter One, I joined the Jesuit Order at the age of twenty-four. I went into the novitiate (a two-year initiatory program to discern, in fact, if one has a vocation) with a load of guilt from past sins. Many were the days I sat at prayer and wondered how I ever got to the Jesuits. Previously, I had been living a life full of distractions from my faith. In the very midst of my desultory way of life, God had spoken in my heart and somehow I had heard. It is still a mystery to me. I recall driving home one Friday afternoon from work and stopping at the local parish to go to confession, a sacrament I had avoided for awhile. As I sat in the pew reciting the penance the priest had given me, my attention was caught by the color of the wall behind the altar. It was light blue. A sense of peace overcame me as I gazed at the wall. At the time I was everywhere but at peace within myself. So affected was I by the inner peace I felt that I began stopping at the church now and then, after work, just to sit and look at the blue wall. Each time, I felt the peace. It wasn't my awareness of Jesus in the tabernacle that drew me, that would come later, but the sereneness of my surroundings. I trace the beginning of my vocation back to those visits. God, it seemed, wasn't holding my past transgressions against me. What a marvel! Now, I look back and realize how significant those days were for me: God not only loved me unconditionally, but invited me to be a disciple! Amazing!

God is not only unlimited in his love, but also endlessly creative in his approaches to us. As a retreat presenter I hear a lot of "come-back" stories, people whose faith life took on new meaning through Cursillo or Marriage Encounter, for example. I have listened to men and women who attend Alcoholics Anonymous tell of meeting God at the very worst time of their life. One friend shared how he experienced God's merciful love, liberating him from a habit of sin that plagued him for many years, by giving him the strength to resist temptations when they arose. Others have shared how the sacrament of reconciliation was a graced experience.

God sees potential for greatness in each of his children. We are like young trees when he finds us. God rescues these "saplings," tends us with care until we become like giant oaks, rooted in his love, our branches full of life for others. Jesus displays God's "reckless love" in washing the feet of the apostles at the Last Supper (John 13:1-17). It is important to keep in mind when reflecting on this passage that Jesus washed the feet of all twelve. Even Judas had his feet washed. Judas, who Jesus knew was going to betray him! Use your imagination to pray with this passage according to the method I briefly described in Chapter One. As you engage in this prayer, pause after each sentence and let the scene unfold. The important thing is to let Jesus wash your feet. Like Peter, you may experience some resistance; if so, ask God to free you so that you can fully receive the love Jesus wishes to give.

Forgiving Oneself

For some people, the most challenging aspect of mercy is the freedom to forgive oneself for something of which one is ashamed. As a priest, when I hear someone in confession naming a sin that he acknowledges he had confessed at a previous time, I automatically assume that he has not forgiven himself for some of the transgression. God not only forgives but forgets what we repented of earlier.

What is it, within our heart, that puts greater demands on us than God does? Is it self-doubt or pride? Is it lack of confidence in our remorse or a need to be perfect always? Father Eamon Tobin suggests "inner tapes" or "voices" may be the root cause of our difficulty, a multitude of "shoulds" that we unconsciously internalized as children. He writes:

> The presence of these tapes causes many of us to have a strong perfectionistic and rigid streak which is very intolerant of our own (and others') mistakes, imperfections, and sins. Often the "inner tape" will represent a parental figure who was very demanding of us—someone maybe long deceased but who is still very alive in our mental processes.[4]

These bothersome "voices" are sometimes referred to as the "Inner Critic," the "Inner Adversary," or the "Inner Tyrant." Fr. Tobin explains:

> They are called *Critic* because they censure so much. They are called *Adversary* because they are like an inner enemy. They are called *Tyrant* because they hold parts of our lives in bondage like a tyrant holds his people in bondage.[5]

If we are to become truly adult in our faith—both in God and in ourselves—we need to learn to say a firm no to these inner "demons." Just as we may have learned how to speak forthrightly to some domineering person in our life, we need to speak directly to our limiting "inner parent." Perhaps the following prayer exercise will further the growth you seek.[6] To facilitate the experience, find a quiet place. Imagine Jesus, walking slowly toward you. Now listen to him as he speaks these words:

> Hi, (*your name*), I have come to be with you for a little while. I have come with good news that I hope you will believe and receive into your heart. I have known you, (*your name*), for all eternity. I know your total history. I know every word you have spoken and every deed you have done. I know your strength and your weakness. I know every single one of your faults, failings, and imperfections, and yet I love you as if you had none of these faults, failings, and imperfections. You see, I am God, and my love for you has no relationship to your behavior. Even if you fail to respond to me and others, I will continue to love you. (*Your name*), you see, "my problem" is that I cannot but love you. If I stopped loving you unconditionally for

one moment, I would no longer be God. I am so different from those perfectionistic voices inside of you. They love you when you perform well. When you perform poorly, they are angry with you. I urge you to stop listening to those voices. They are destructive. They are not of me, even though they sometimes try to parrot my voice. It is crucial that you learn to distinguish my voice from the voice of your "Inner Critic," "Adversary," and "Tyrant." My voice is never harsh, judgmental, or condemning. It is gentle, inviting, compassionate, and full of mercy. All I seek is for you to believe that I love you. Once you believe that, loving words and deeds will flow from your being into the world. . . .

Some people mistakenly think that all this talk about my love only gives them a license to do whatever they want. They think that because I love them so much, it doesn't matter what they do. Those who have that attitude may have heard about my love, but they certainly haven't *experienced* it in the depths of their hearts.

(*Your name*), please ponder (as Mary pondered my Word in her heart) these words I have spoken to you. Do not just read them quickly and move on. *Take time* to allow my words to touch your heart so that they become words that will form your image of me.

Do I confuse God's voice with other voices within me? Do I truly believe in God's merciful love for me?

It takes courage to forgive oneself, to show compassion and mercy in the face of self-blame. It is what one author calls "love's ultimate daring."[7] However, forgiving oneself is necessary if we are to recapture the realization of God's complete love for us, God's unconditional love.

Terry, an accountant in his mid-forties, shares how he has learned from experience not to be too harsh with himself: "My image of God as kind and loving brought me to find more forgiveness in my heart for myself. I am now better able to accept my shortcomings and find contentment with all the blessings I have been given. An inner peace has come to me over time as I have learned to accept who I am and what is truly important in my life."

Kathy, whose early life image of God was that of a judge, has found some relief in her new found experience of God: "Knowing that God knows me as no one else can helps me to be more forgiving of myself, though I still find myself at times falling into my old pattern of trying to meet some impossible moral standard."

Perhaps this is her "Inner Tyrant" at work.

To complete the process of self-forgiveness, Lewis Smedes suggests making a "reckless act of love," for love is the proof that the guilt which condemned us is gone. A stirring example of this in the New Testament is related in Luke's gospel:

> A Pharisee invited Jesus to have dinner with him, and Jesus went to his house and sat down to eat. In that town was a woman who lived a sinful life. She heard that Jesus was eating in the Pharisee's house, so she brought an alabaster jar full of perfume and stood behind Jesus, by his feet, crying and wetting his feet with her tears. Then she

dried his feet with her hair, kissed them, and poured perfume on them (7:36-38).

Professor Smedes comments on this story:

> She loves much because she has been forgiven much—this was Jesus' explanation for a woman who dared to barge into a dinner party uninvited, plunk herself at Jesus' feet, and pour out a small cascade of love. . . . A free act of love, to anyone at all, may signal to you that you do, after all, have the power that comes to anyone who is self-forgiving.[8]

When I joined the Jesuits I did so with a lot of inner baggage. One of my suitcases was full of guilt for past mistakes, especially in the area of sexuality. I had led a very active social life and dated all through high school and college. In the novitiate, I became acutely aware of the sinfulness of my past. Paradoxically, this is when I also discovered a God who forgives completely, unconditionally. Still, it took quite awhile before I was able to even entertain the possibility of having women friends as a Jesuit. Looking back, I see I needed to forgive myself for what I had done, to come to terms with what one of my spiritual advisors called my "overdeveloped super ego," and to learn to trust myself. Though this process took ten years, my "reckless act of love" came when I finally allowed myself to become friends with a woman. Not only did we share similar values, but she was physically beautiful as well, which warmed my Italian heart! I had come full circle, but from license to real freedom. All, I believe, because of the incredible love I had received from God who never gave up on me.

Catholics know they have forgiven themselves when they no longer feel the need to confess some particular sin again. All of us know we have emerged from the tyranny of self-blame when we feel at one with ourselves, at peace. As Lewis Smedes explains, "The split is healed. The self inside you, who condemned you so fiercely, embraces you now. You are whole, single; you have come together."[9] This is not an arrogant or conceited gesture, this forgiving of oneself. You have faced the wrong you did with a firm desire not to repeat it, but you refuse to let this "old" part of yourself dictate who you are now. You have learned to love yourself unconditionally as God loves you.

Unconditional Love

There must be no limit to my confidence in God's love. Most of us learn this truth over time as we reflect on our God-experiences and as we discover that God wishes only our good even though the good sometimes involves the cross. It took two years for the significance of God's love for me to really sink in. Besides discovering the love of God in my prayer, I learned to see his love in people and things around me. For example, at Christmas I would read each card that arrived as not only coming from a friend but also from God who had given me this friend. I did this for years as a way to deepen the initial grace.

"The essential message of unconditional love is one of liberation," writes Father John Powell. "You can be whoever you are, express all your thoughts and feelings with absolute confidence. You do not have to be fearful that love will be taken away."[10] In the Old Testament we see this kind of love in the way King David is treated by God. Despite David's severe moral lapse (2 Samuel 11), God sends Nathan the prophet to "wake" David up and bring him to repentance. When David admits his guilt, God does not remove him from his kingship but liberates him from his moral blindness.[11]

An example from the New Testament of this kind of love appears in the story of the two disciples on their way home to Emmaus after Jesus' crucifixion (see Luke 24:13-35). Unlike the other disciples who stayed in Jerusalem, albeit hidden for fear of the Jewish authorities, these two had given up, were in despair. As they walked along Jesus joined them, though they did not know it was him. He asked them what they were talking about. When with great sadness they explained, he did not condemn their lack of understanding nor despair of them. Instead, he patiently led them through the books of Moses and the writings of the prophets until they understood. It was then that they had the necessary faith to recognize him as they realized that he had the power to rise from the dead.

God has a way of meeting us, in various disguises, and showering upon us love unimaginable. We need our eyes opened occasionally to take it all in. A prayer exercise I often use on retreats gives us just such an opportunity. It is called "Experiencing the Vastness of God's Love."[12]

> Imagine you are standing atop a high mountain. As you look through the clouds below, you see a limitless canyon, a vast abyss. No one can measure its height or depth. You stand in amazement at the scene below you.
>
> You glimpse the beginnings of a gentle white light. You sense someone moving toward you—someone who emanates safety, security, and wonder. An angel steps before you. The angel takes your hand. Your heart is full of wonder and a sense of being safe. You stand there awhile, drifting even further into calmness. The clouds begin to glitter with a

sparkling light, a light that dazzles you and warms you at the same time. You sense that the angel wants you to jump with him into the vast canyon below. The angel tells you that this is the canyon of the height and depth of God's love.

How do you feel as you contemplate jumping into the canyon? Perhaps fear—fear of the unknown. Perhaps worry—worry that if you are surrounded by so much love, you will lose your identity. Or, perhaps, you feel a yearning, a longing to experience the inconceivable love that awaits you down below.

Do not jump until you are ready. You may wish to ask God for the courage and the trust to jump.

When you jump, you feel so light as you float through the sparkling clouds with the angel. Ways of feeling, ways of seeing that have always been within you but unknown to you come alive. You sense a love that is beyond anything you have experienced before, a measureless joy, a vibrant aliveness that cannot be expressed in words. A sweetness fills the inner spaces of your heart. The light is so bright that you close your eyes, and still the light shines through your closed eyelids. How weightless and free you feel floating in this endless cloud of light.

As you float, the deep clouds pass on to you the love of God. God's loving energy flows to every cell of your body. Every cell feels vibrantly alive. You are bathed in a heavenly glow.

You float toward the center, the very center of God's love, toward this light beyond all light. You experience yourself as being completely and unconditionally loved.

Rest in this experience of infinite love and glowing warmth. Let the love of God permeate your whole being.

When it is time to return to earth and to your place in it, you thank God in some way for this extraordinary experience of love. You are at peace in your inmost self.

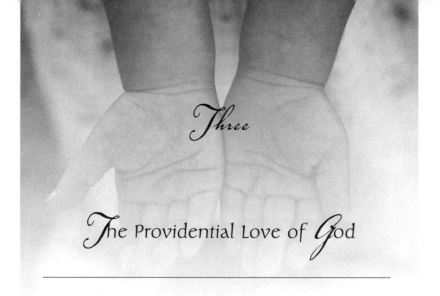

Three

The Providential Love of God

The divine action, although only visible to the eye of faith, is everywhere, and always present.[1]

JEAN PIERRE DE
CAUSSADE

My mother was diagnosed with cancer at the age of forty-four. I was eighteen and in my second year of college. My brother was one year old, there are three sisters in between my brother and me. During the two years that our mother struggled with this deadly disease, I would notice during my vacations home a book by her bed. The book was called *Abandonment to Divine Providence*, the author an eighteenth-century French Jesuit by the name of Jean Pierre de Caussade. I didn't fully realize the significance of this book for my mother until six years later. I was in the Jesuit novitiate by then, and one day I was browsing in the house library. I came across Fr. de Caussade's book and began to read it. Not only did his book have a profound impact on me, it gave me new insight into my mother and the depth of her faith.

Many nurses and doctors told our family that they considered mom to be a saint. For one thing, though often in a lot of pain, she never complained. The other striking feature was her complete inner peace despite the fact that in dying she would leave my dad with five children. Reading de Caussade's book, which stresses total surrender to God by trusting in his loving providence, it became clear to me the source of this gift God had given mom. She trusted God completely, and believed that he would indeed take care of our family. She died peacefully on Easter Sunday morning, two years after learning of the cancer.

The challenge for someone facing death as my mother did is not only to totally trust in God's providential love but to keep loving God in return while one's body is being ravaged by sickness and one's family and friends are beside themselves with grief. As the great Rabbi Akiba, who died as a martyr, said as he approached death, "'Thou shalt love the Lord your God with all your heart, with all your soul, and with all your might' means you are to love God even if He takes your life!"[2]

Not all of our experiences of trusting in God's providence lead to death, of course. Here are two stories where, in fact, the opposite occurred. First, Bev shares a bit about his life:

> I was born, and I lived because my grandmother was visiting our family and knew how to solve a physical problem that even the doctors couldn't handle. As a young aspiring engineer on a dam site, one day I moved from a spot where seconds later several workers were swept to their deaths. Later, I encountered many bears and other threatening wild-life in the course of geological duties in the Canadian bush. A few years after my wife, Diane, and I were married, I

survived a horrendous helicopter crash in Alaska. God only knows how many other similar instances of possible injury, or death, could have happened to me. But I am still alive.

Surely this speaks of God's caring, of his having a purpose for me, and of his hope that I be the kind of person he wants me to be. How can I do anything else with my life than to try and please him?

Joyce relates an incident of God's loving concern that came at a time in which she was feeling especially low:

My mother suffered a stroke shortly after our second child was born. We lived clear across town from my parents so helping my dad with her care was pretty tough. To make matters worse, I was caught in the crossfire between the two men in my life. My father thought I wasn't doing enough to help my mother while my husband thought I was spending too much time looking after her and not enough with our two children and him. This stressful situation went on for two years. By that time, I was feeling pretty useless on all counts of my life, so much so that I was seriously considering ending my life.

What saved me happened one Sunday afternoon at a family picnic. My husband and I took the children to the countryside, to a place that has a river running through it. My husband and the children walked down a steep bank to play by the river while I stood at the top of the bank. I felt very removed from the joy the three of them were experiencing. I remember pointing out to God that they would be fine without me and I asked him why if I was so unnecessary and useless to everyone that I was created in the first place. At that moment of deep sadness, without any conscious effort on my part, my head turned towards a small clearing near where I was standing. At the far end of the clearing were some tall solid spruce trees, which would normally be the focus of sight. However, the vision I was given was of a tiny clump of some small edelweiss-type flowers growing at the base of one of these huge trees. The trees became fuzzy to my eyes but the little flowers, which were some distance away, became so clear that I was able to see each grain of pollen, each vein in the leaves. The way the flowers were nourished and grew was shown to me. And, most important, I was shown *how* the flowers were created. I was shown the *love* with which each of the flowers were created: the care, the joy, the love, and the Creator's wonder at that which he had created. And, while God was showing me all this, he said to me: "Look at the love with which I created this small flower. If I created a small flower with such infinite care and love, believe that I created you, Joyce, with an even greater love. You are precious in my sight and glorious."

Have you had similar experiences of God's providence?

In his book, Fr. de Caussade points out that there is not a moment in which God is not present to us in his providence, both in our joyful and in our difficult times. God is really and truly with us, invisible but for the eyes of faith and so we are always surprised when we recognize his hand. Fr. de Caussade writes:

> If we could lift the veil, and if we were attentive and watchful, God would continually reveal himself to us, and we should see his divine action in everything that happened to us and rejoice in it. At each successive occurrence we should exclaim: "It is the Lord!"[3]

I am reminded here of *The Celestine Prophecy*, in which the author writes of "mysterious coincidences" in our lives. In the book the reader follows the adventures of a young man and woman as they seek answers to life's basic questions; these are to be found, in the story, in an ancient manuscript which is composed of nine insights. In the following dialogue between the man and the woman, we get a glimpse into the first insight. The priest referred to is another character in the story.

> "Okay," I said. "What is this experience we're looking for? What is the First Insight?"
>
> She hesitated, as though unsure how to begin. "This is hard to explain," she said. "But the priest put it this way. He said the First Insight occurs when we become conscious of the *coincidences* in our lives."
>
> "Well," she continued, "according to the priest, these coincidences are happening more and more frequently and that, when they do, they strike us as beyond what would be expected by pure chance. They feel destined, as though our lives had been guided by some unexplained force. The

experience induces a feeling of mystery and excitement and, as a result, we feel more alive. . . ."

"Don't you see?" she asked. "The First Insight is a reconsideration of the inherent mystery that surrounds our individual lives on this planet. We are experiencing these mysterious coincidences, and even though we don't understand them yet, we know they are real. We are sensing again, as in childhood, that there is another side of life that we have yet to discover, some other process operating behind the scenes."[4]

Allow me to illustrate the above lesson by a personal story. As part of my Jesuit training, in 1977 I went to Calcutta, India to live for three months. I stayed with the Brothers of the Missionaries of Charity, at their novitiate, and worked with them at Mother Teresa's Home for Dying Destitutes and other places that serve the poor. As I was preparing to leave my home in Berkeley, California for India, I encountered some fear within myself. I had heard stories about the severity of the poverty in Calcutta, that there were thousands of people living on the sidewalks. My anxiety centered on who would be there that I could talk to about what I would be experiencing. As an extrovert, I knew I would either go crazy or give up and come home early if I did not have people to share with.

I arrived at the Calcutta airport at midnight and was welcomed by the Novice Master. As we drove through the city, I saw many families sleeping by the side of the road and on sidewalks. On the second day after I arrived, the Brothers took me to the Home for Dying Destitutes, the first place that Mother Teresa founded. I saw immediately that this was in no way a hospital, but a place where people were brought, too poor to go to a hospital, to die with dignity. I was given a pitcher of water, a pan, and a towel and proceeded to the first order of the day—washing the bodies of those in the men's ward. Each man had his own cot. As I slowly made my way from one man to the next, I was aware of how terribly thin each was. My fingers touched bones as I carefully soaped and rinsed these emaciated people. At mid-morning we had a break and were asked to come back in half an hour to help feed the men. I walked over to a spot by the entrance and stood for a few minutes reading a prayer that was hanging from one of the pillars there.

I could see into the men's area from where I stood, could see some of the men I had recently washed. Suddenly, tears started rolling down my cheeks. I knew I could not continue working there that day and motioned to one of the other volunteers. He seemed to understand my reaction to the suffering around us and agreed to take me back to the Brothers' House, a bus ride away. Brother Andrew, then General Servant of the Brothers, was visiting at the time and he invited me to have a cup of tea with him. As I sat with him and began giving him an account of the morning, I completely broke down and cried till I had no tears left. He simply sat with me and supported me by his presence. Finally, he suggested I take a few days off, get to know the city a bit, and then let him know if I wanted to return to the Home for Dying Destitutes or go somewhere else.

During those two days, the fear I had felt before leaving home about not having people to talk to about what I was seeing and experiencing resurfaced. I felt comfortable with Brother Andrew, but he was due to leave Calcutta soon. On the second day, I joined the Brothers at Mass. Brother Andrew was the celebrant. The gospel was on the multiplication of the loaves and fish. In his homily, Brother Andrew commented on the fact that after everyone had eaten there was still food left over. "What this means to me," he said, "is that God provides not only what we need but more than we need to do his work." This insight jolted me as I realized it contained the answer to my fears. I had to believe that God would provide what I needed—people to share with—and even more than I would need to help me process my feelings and thoughts during my time in Calcutta. And that is precisely what did happen. I met people throughout the summer, in various places, who helped me make sense of what I was going through in order to integrate it. Was it merely a coincidence that the reading at Mass and Brother Andrew's reflections were exactly what I needed to hear on that particular day or was something much more profound at work here? One thing for sure, my trust in God's providence deepened enormously that summer and I have never forgotten the lesson I learned, that when God asks us to do something we will be provided not only with what we need to accomplish it, but even more than we need.

Footprints

As we saw in Chapter One, the image of God in us is primarily a potential to take in the love of God. One essential avenue to fulfilling this potential is being attentive to the ways God is loving and providing for us. Sometimes, like in the story of my mother, our awareness of God's presence is ongoing; other times it is not until we look back on an experience that we see God's mark.

Margaret's story about her and her husband is an example. She tells it in her own words:

The story of how I met Larry after receiving my annulment shows God working in my life. Coming from different parts of the country, how we both ended up in the same city and at a Catholic singles club meeting we feel was God's hand in our lives.

In like manner, Audrey was in her early twenties and had three young children from a previous marriage when she met Bob. She credits the Creator for this encounter: "God certainly works in strange ways, to meet a man of Bob's caliber, a man willing to take on the responsibility of an immediate family." They celebrated their twenty-fifth wedding anniversary last year.

Mary Ann also reflects on how she sees God's purpose in her life. She married at the age of forty-two.

With maturity, I think we believe in and become more aware of God's love for us. As time passes, and I am able to look back over my life, I am acutely aware of how God has so carefully guided my every step. When I was younger I prayed for such gifts as a happy, healthy, and holy marriage. I look back now and realize that Our Lord was preparing me for Denny. Had he and I met years earlier, I would not have been prepared for the magnificent gift of our union. I see that the Lord led me away from relationships that were unhealthy or unfulfilling, helping me, at the same time, to grow in my understanding and appreciation of what a good marriage requires. Indeed, I needed to become more confident, more trusting, less judgmental, and less selfish in order to be able to contribute to a marriage.

In the words of the Psalmist, these three women could exclaim, "The Lord has done great things for us; we are glad indeed" (126:3 NAB).

Who are the people in your life who incarnate or make real God's care for you?

Many people, from all walks of life and all religions have drawn comfort and inspiration from the reflection "Footprints" by an anonymous author; it is truly a reminder to us of God's providence.

> One night a man had a dream. He dreamed he was walking along the beach with the Lord. Across the sky flashed scenes from his life. For each scene, he noticed two sets of footprints in the sand; one belonging to him, and the other to the Lord. When the last scene of his life flashed before him, he looked back at the footprints in the sand. He noticed that many times along the path of his life there was only one set of footprints. He also noticed that it happened at the very lowest and saddest times in his life. This really bothered him and he questioned the Lord about it. "Lord, you said that once I decided to follow you, you'd walk with me all the way. But I have noticed that during the most troublesome times in my life, there is only one set of footprints. I don't understand why when I needed you most you would leave me." The Lord replied, "My precious child, I love you and I would never leave you. During your times of trial and suffering, when you see only one set of footprints, it was then that I carried you.

Susan, a friend of mine, shares how this reflection affects her: "'Footprints in the Sand,' helps me to see the different ways God loves me, that he always walks beside me and carries me especially when I am feeling weak due to life's circumstances. Often, as the poem says, I do not recognize God in my life until I look back."

In like manner, Terry finds consolation through "Footprints" as he reflects on why he knows and believes in God's love for him:

When I look back over periods of my life, I come to the realization that I was not alone in whatever I was going through. Sometimes it was people who provided support to me or circumstances mysteriously worked out or the answer I was seeking came "magically." I am now in mid-life and I have many blessings to thank God for. I have a marriage of twenty-nine years where my wife and I still love and care for each other. We have two nearly grown men as children who make us very proud. We have family who we care deeply for and who care for us. We are part of a faith community where we are free to worship and share in the love of God. We have friendships that span thirty years. We have a small family business that provides for all our needs and allows us to share some of our good fortune with others. We have our health. All these things have not just happened. We have lived through some difficult times; we have needed help to get through them, the help has always been there. At times, it may have appeared to be a coincidence that something worked out. I believe God has had a hand in making things happen. Hence, my appreciation of "Footprints."

Personal and Communal Experiences

In addition to looking back over one's life in order
to see the providential presence of God, there are
those everyday experiences in which we know there
is more than mere coincidence operating.

Sr. Celine Millette is a Sister of Providence. She is
ninety years old and lived on the Siksika (Blackfoot)
Reserve, in southern Alberta, Canada, for a total of
fifty-two years. She recently told me a story of something that happened about a year ago. She told me
how she drove herself and a woman from the reserve
a fair distance from the convent in order to pick
berries. While her friend went about the business of
berry picking, Sr. Celine thought about the youth of
the community and prayed for them as she recited her
rosary. When it came time to leave, the car would not
start. This startled and frightened the two women for
there were no houses in the vicinity and dusk was
descending. Just then two cars drove by, each full of
teenagers! They passed by, but then one of the youth
said let's go back and see Sr. Celine whose car they
had recognized. When sister explained their predica-
ment, one of the drivers went in search of help while
the other car and occupants stayed with sister and her
friend until all was well. "It was the Lord's work,"
Sister said to me with complete conviction, "they
didn't even know we were in trouble until I told them.
And, amazingly, help came through the very
age-group I had just been praying for. It was God's
providence at work."

In 1990, I experienced three significant personal
losses in the space of one month: my father died, my
siblings decided to sell the home we grew up in, and
the new pastor of the parish where I had been living
for three good years decided to renovate the rectory
and asked me to move. I was walking around in a

daze of grief for the losses and insecurity as to where I would live. Toward the end of that month, I decided to pay a last visit to our home, before it was sold. I still had my key. Unfortunately, I had forgotten about the auctioning of the furniture. When I walked into the house, I was emotionally devastated by the empty rooms that I encountered. There was absolutely nothing left in the den where Dad and I had often visited. In the living room, where our family had celebrated many a Christmas and other festive occasions, a mattress leaning against the wall was the only object in the room. I had had enough, I was not going to compound my misery by going upstairs. I was to meet an old friend of the family for dinner but had a couple of hours before that engagement. I needed space. My emotions were in turmoil. Nowhere in the previous month had I had a sense of God being present, least of all at that moment as I left the house for the last time.

I drove till I found a park. As I prepared to get out of the car, I remembered there was a book in the back seat which a friend had recently given to me. I had not yet opened the book. I took it with me into the park and sat on a bench. I find it hard to believe, even now, the "oddness" of the book's author and its title: *The Joy of Full Surrender*, by Jean Pierre de Caussade! It is an updated translation of his classic work on abandonment. I opened to the section entitled, "Trials Connected with the State of Full Surrender," feeling without a doubt that I was in the middle of a full-blown trial of my faith. Within minutes of opening the book, I read the following sentence: "We are troubled and disturbed, yet nevertheless in our depths we have some unseen anchor that keeps us clinging to God."[5]

Suddenly, my eyes were opened and I had a strong sense of God's presence; that my faith, though it seemed to me quite dim over the previous month, was still very much alive, an "unseen anchor." Here, in the midst of one of my lowest life moments, God provided me with a tangible assurance that all was not lost.

Then I read a paragraph that put my trial in perspective.

> To live by faith is to live by joy, confidence, and certainty about all that has to be done or suffered at each moment by God's will. It is in order to animate and to maintain this life of faith that God allows us to be plunged into and carried away by the rough waters of numerous pains, troubles, difficulties, weaknesses and defeats. *For it requires faith to find God in all these* [emphasis mine]. The divine life is given to us at every moment in a hidden but very sure way, under different appearances. . . . In all these, faith finds its nourishment and strength. It pierces through them all and clings to the hand of God, the Giver of life.[6]

There are many images to accompany these stories of God's providence: the child being cupped in God's hand, sitting on God's lap, resting in the boat after Jesus calmed the storm, to name a few. "I see myself as a child comfortably resting in God's arms," shares Betty, "sitting on a park bench with him or walking by a river hand in hand." "I feel God's touch when he hugs me, I feel him wipe away my tears, I feel him take my hand and walk with me; I am not alone," shares Theresa.

Sr. Therese Monaghan wrote the following beautiful meditation, an apt reflection on the providence of God; it is based on the scripture passage, "We walk by faith, not by sight" (2 Corinthians 5:7 NAB).

You draw us.
Step by step
Snail-like we find our way
Through brush and mud and grassy field.
We skirt the rocks and crags
And fall in unexpected holes

And then . . . you lift us
And we see the stars.
As eagles soar, we thrill
To build your world on further shore
And dare to reach beyond ourselves.
But with warm wisdom
You let us walk again
To pass through mist
And feel the dark
And stumble on your Presence
With incremental glimpses of your promised
    land.
You strengthen us with human bonds
And nourish us with sweet and bitter food along
    the way.
We are rich in promise and fulfillment.
We walk by faith and not by sight.

Oh, Love Divine
Draw us further.
You have refined us for another shore.
Take us beyond our narrow sight
To where the path is brighter, clearer.
Or is it, you tell us,
That we travel with an inner sight
And, like falling leaves,
Can meet the earth with lighter, smaller steps
To build your world.
We walk by faith and not by sight.[7]

It is possible, also, to experience God's providence in a communal way. A few examples come to mind: the Second Vatican Council came at a time when the Catholic church was in need of a transformation; many parishes have been changed for the better by the Renew Program; over the past thirty years most religious orders have found ways to rediscover their original charism in order to apply it more effectively to the times. Each of these metamorphoses can be seen through the prism of providence.

My friends Bob and Audrey Breaker shared with me a way in which God's providence came to the people of the Blackfoot community in southern Alberta, Canada. In the 1960s the Canadian government gave aboriginal people the right to buy liquor. This led to a lot of alcoholism on the reserves which had a devastating effect, not only on individual people and their families but also on the whole community. Like the Israelite people in the Old Testament, concerned members of the Blackfoot nation cried to God for help. The first sign that God had heard them came in the form of Cursillo, a three-day short course in Christianity conducted by lay people. It was a tremendous source of moral conversion for many. Prayer groups began forming after each Cursillo in people's homes and the youth got involved in Searches and other kinds of weekend Christian retreats. "Pilgrimages" also emerged from Cursillo. A Pilgrimage is a four-day experience for people who are struggling with addictions, especially to alcohol or drugs. Like Cursillo, it is a combination of talks based on the lived experiences of the presenters, shared reflections, socials, and most importantly the celebration of the eucharist. A Pilgrimage can be made as often as needed so that the total healing sought by each participant may eventually be theirs. As a result of these various healing and retreat movements, many people were led from fear, self-doubt, and lack of appreciation of themselves to greater self-confidence and experiences of the joy of being followers of Jesus. One can easily see God's providential hand in this.

God's Sense of Humor

All is not serious in this "providence business," as the following two accounts illustrate.

A couple of years ago, while giving parish missions in southern Alberta, Canada, I developed a problem in my upper back. The difficulty began in December of that year when I lifted a box of books in such a way that two vertebrae were adversely affected. I will go more deeply into this experience in the chapter on God's healing love. What I want to highlight here is something that happened three months later in the middle of Lent. I had returned to the Calgary diocese to give parish missions. My back was still bothering and preoccupying me. During the first mission, I met a man who had a men's clothing store. As I had two pairs of pants that needed alterations, I decided to go to his shop to have the work done after the mission. In the intervening time, I was at a dinner party in a town west of Calgary and told the story of how I had met this fellow and my intention of going to his store. One of the guests exclaimed, "That's where I buy my shirts! Ask him when my newly ordered shirts will arrive." I thought, what an interesting coincidence.

Before I go any further in this story, the reader should know that I love getting things for free or at a reduced rate; this pleases me no end and always lifts my spirits. I have met many people with a similar disposition; perhaps it has something to do with living in a materialistic culture. Anyway, off I went then to the men's store, pants in hand. The owner greeted

me warmly. "Of course, I can alter the pants for you,
Father, and there will be no charge." Great news, I
thought! I told him about his customer that I had met
at the dinner gathering. He exclaimed, "Yes, I know
the man well, he's been coming to my store for years.
Just the other day, however, he returned a beautiful
blue shirt that was just a bit too big for him. Wait, I'll
show you." He went into the back room and returned
holding up an expensive looking long-sleeve shirt. He
then looked at me more closely and said, "You and
this fellow are the same height and build! Tell you
what, I'll give you this shirt, no charge. I'll have it
pressed and ready for you when you come to pick up
the pants." Wow! I thought, another freebie; regardless of my back problems, my spirits were soaring as
a result of this man's generosity.

Four days later, I returned to the store to collect
my pants and the new shirt. We chatted a bit, the
owner and I. I told him I was on my way to the south
of the diocese, a trip that would take a couple of hours
in the car. It was cold and snowy outside so I had my
gloves with me. As I prepared to leave, the owner saw
my gloves, rather large ones but warm for the hands.
He looked at me with concern and said, "Are you
going to drive with those gloves on?" When I nodded
yes, he replied, "Father, I worry about you, those
gloves are not for driving, they are for playing in the
snow. Wait a minute," he said as he turned to a shelf
behind him and came back with a tray of light,
leather, gloves. Expensive, I thought. "Here, try this
pair on." I obliged. They felt great and even smelled
leathery. And they fit me perfectly. "I want you to
have these gloves," he said. "I'll feel a whole lot better
if you drive with them on rather than those other
bulky ones." Just then the pants and pressed shirt
arrived from the back room. I walked out of his store,
happier than I had been since before my back started

bothering me. Amazing, pants altered: no charge! A brand new shirt: free! And, to top it all, a new pair of gloves! What a generous guy. What a marvelous God, to provide such a delightful distraction at a time of physical distress.

Sister Anne Smollin recounts the following humorous story in her book, *Tickle Your Soul*. The experience she relates is what pushed her to finish this writing project.

> One day that was more hectic than most provided the final shove that made me take the time to complete this volume. I had several client appointments [she is a family counselor], and sandwiched in between them were two workshops and a dinner keynote address. The day before had been even more pressured. So when I jumped in my car after having seen five clients and given the first workshop to a hospice group on "Wellness and Humor," I began feeling very tired. Trying to ignore this feeling, because I still had to see one more client and then give the dinner address, I steered my car onto the New York State Thruway and began talking out loud to myself. I asked myself why I was working so hard and why I was accepting more speaking commitments. I began to talk about the unfinished projects I had not gotten to. Then I engaged God in my conversation: "God, why am I doing all of this? What should I do and what should I let go of? You know, God, I do enjoy working, and I love all the lectures I give. But I can't keep up this pace much longer. And what about that book? Should I finish it or should I just forget the whole thing? God, if only you would help. If only you could send me a sign, then

I would know what I really should be
doing."

As I said these words, I looked at the truck in
front of me. The back panel of the truck read:
G.O.D. Call 1-800-DIAL-GOD. I got hysteri-
cal. I was laughing so loudly that I thought if
anyone looked at me, they would certainly
question my mental status. The "Guaranteed
Overnight Delivery" truck had delivered my
answer, and I began to put my energies into
completing this book.[8]

Have you experienced God's sense of humor?
How?

Old Testament Providence

The entire account of Yahweh and Israel is really a
story about God's providence. From the Exodus to the
covenant and to the prophets, God is continually caring for his people. Whether it's by means of manna in
the wilderness or the castigation of Isaiah, or one of
God's other messengers, each speaks of a divine being
who is involved with people and not aloof. "Then the
Lord said, 'I have seen how cruelly my people are
being treated in Egypt; I have heard them cry out to
be rescued from their slave drivers. I know all about
their sufferings, and so I have come down to rescue
them from the Egyptians and to bring them out of
Egypt to a fertile and spacious land . . .'" (Exodus 3:7-
8a). Using nature images, the Psalmist reflects on this
relationship:

> You brought a grapevine out of Egypt;
> you drove out other nations
>   and planted it in their land.
> You cleared a place for it to grow;

its roots went deep, and it
> spread out over the whole land . . .
> (80:8-9).

Isaiah, too, speaks of the Beloved caring and providing for the loved ones as a winegrower does for the harvest:

Listen while I sing you this song,
a song of my friend and his vineyard;
My friend had a vineyard on a very fertile
hill.
He dug the soil and cleared it of stones;
He planted the finest vines.
He built a tower to guard them,
> dug a pit for treading the grapes.
He waited for the grapes to ripen . . .
> (5:1-2).

After the people have returned from the exile, God once again displays his concern for the people with an age-image that can be comforting to us as well.

Listen to me, descendants of Jacob,
all who are left of my people.
I have cared for you from the time you were
born.
I am your God and will take care of you
until you are old and your hair is gray.
I made you and will care for you;
I will give you help and rescue you
> (Isaiah 46:3-4).

Living as I do, among aboriginal people, the image of God that now most captures my imagination is the eagle. The Song of Moses in the book of Deuteronomy describes God as caring for the Israelite people in the following manner: "Like an eagle teaching its young to fly, catching them safely on its spreading wings, the Lord kept Israel from falling" (32:11).

For North American aboriginal people, the eagle is a symbol of leadership. Writes Ed McGaa, Eagle Man, "It is the creature symbol of greatest power because it flies so high, close to the Great Spirit, and is regarded as the eyes of the all-seeing powers of *Wakan Tanka*, the one above who created all things."[9] In the song "On Eagle's Wings," by Michael Joncas, the refrain is rich in this image.

To some Native Americans the eagle is associated with Waburn, Spirit Keeper of the East, representing rebirths, innocence, and eternal spring.[10] Each of these are wonderful symbols of God's loving providence.

Conclusion

An excellent way to conclude this chapter is with St. Ignatius' *Suscipe* Prayer ("Take and Receive"), for it recognizes who we are as human beings, who the Giver of all good gifts is, and what our grateful response might be.

Take, Lord, and receive all my liberty,
my memory, my understanding, and my
entire will—all that I have and call my own.
You have given it all to me.
To you, Lord, I return it.
Everything is yours;
do with it what you will.
Give me only your love and your grace.
That is enough for me.[11]

four

The Freeing Love of *God*

Have faith in God. I assure you that whoever
tells this hill to get up and throw itself in the
sea and does not doubt in [their] heart, but
believes that what [they] say will happen, it
will be done for [them].

MARK 11:22-23

As I enter into my sixties and look back over the past twenty years, I see that my forties were my freest time. It was in my early forties that God gave me a priceless gift, what I call the "freedom-prayer." I have shared this method of prayer in a variety of circumstances: parish missions, weekend retreats, and in spiritual direction. Of all the affirmations in ministry that have come my way in the past twenty years, most have to do with the effectiveness of this prayer for inner freedom in people's lives.

I have learned a lot about the blocks to interior freedom, especially in the areas of excessive emotional needs and fears, and so the following is an updated review of this valuable tool for spiritual growth.

It is important to note at the outset that the kind of faith called for in the freedom-prayer is the faith of a child: an openness and trust. This faith is based on the reality of God's unconditional love for us. Further, I have come to realize more and more that God wants us to be free, wants to heal us of anything that inhibits our freedom to love and be loved. Faith is a gift, but we grow in faith each time we put our trust in God's love. In the gospels, Jesus urges people to have faith and he praises those who do (Matthew 8:10-13). If we have the faith even the size of a tiny mustard seed, God can do wonders in us. The mountain that even faith can move may be a gigantic fear, a relentless resentment, or some other restriction on our freedom to live the kind of life God wishes for us. If we are ready to believe that we will receive whatever we ask for in prayer, we are spiritually prepared to practice the freedom-prayer.

I have found the best way to explain this prayer for inner freedom is to share how it came into my life. In the summer of 1982 I lived and worked among economically poor people in Tijuana, Mexico. I stayed at a multi-service facility for those in need of food, clothing, and medical care, a place where our Jesuit province has been sending novices for short periods as part of their novitiate training. However, I was the only Jesuit there that summer. The people I met ministered to me in many unexpected ways. They helped me get over some prejudices I had toward Mexicans. Through their spontaneous and warm way of relating, they touched my heart so deeply that by the end of the summer I realized I had fallen in love with the people. This effect led to one of the most difficult decisions I have faced as a Jesuit: to ask, or not, my provincial for permission to move to San Diego in order to work part-time across the border. The discernment involved its own encounter with detachment and freedom, for I had lived for fifteen years in northern California and had many close friends as well as family living in the vicinity. I knew few people in the San Diego area and did not yet speak sufficient Spanish to converse easily in it.

One day I was praying about this decision and the image of the rich young man in the gospel of St. Luke came to mind. He had kept the commandments since he was a young boy, but wanted to do more. Jesus said to him: "There is one thing further you must do. Sell all you have and give to the poor. You will have treasure in heaven. Then come and follow me" (18:22, NAB). When I asked myself what do I have to "sell," or let go of, the answer was not so much material things as goods of the heart: a wonderful, supportive Jesuit community, family nearby, and longstanding friendships. With the Spirit's grace, I was able to follow this new invitation from God. I asked for permission to move. Years later I was reminded of this transition by Frank Andersen's poignant, "Galilee Song." The refrain says it all:

> So I leave my boats behind,
> leave them on familiar shores
> set my heart upon the deep,
> follow you again, my Lord.[1]

"Boats" are those things in our lives that provide security. This was literally true for Peter and Andrew, James and John. In my experience, the more we are freed to follow Jesus and leave our boats behind, the deeper the water gets.

What are the boats in your life? Are you being called to leave any of them behind?

While I awaited an answer from the provincial I had the opportunity to return to Tijuana for a visit. There I encountered something unexpected in myself that greatly unsettled me.

On the one hand, it was wonderful to see people I had met during the summer once again, to play with the children, to joke with teenagers, to receive hugs from men and women who had become my friends. However, I found myself emotionally withdrawing at times from them. I did not know why. When I returned home, a sobering question plagued me: how can I move to San Diego in this new emotional state? Is this a sign that I am not supposed to move, I asked myself. In the midst of these deliberations, the provincial phoned to give me permission to move! The following day I began my eight-day annual retreat, and it was on this retreat that the freedom-prayer came into my life.

I was meditating on the annunciation when I began to see the cause of my emotional withdrawal from the people in Tijuana. It was Mary's humility that caught my attention. I recalled that at my recent visit there were two of our novices at the facility. They had been there for over a month. During the summer I had been the only Jesuit living and working there. The novices had become friends with many of the same people I had met during the summer, and they were receiving the same kind of affection I had experienced. Not only that, but they were getting to know my favorite families! All of a sudden, my eyes were opened and I realized the cause of my withdrawal—jealousy. The "apple pie of affection," as I put it, which had been all mine during the summer was now being split three ways! Another person might get angry when jealous; my response was to withdraw emotionally. It was a humiliating realization.

When I shared this insight with the Jesuit directing my retreat, he suggested that I pray for *freedom from the need to be special*, a quality of humility Mary had. I took his advice. Every time I felt the tendency to withdraw because of jealous feelings, I simply said the words, "Lord, please free me from the need to be special." The feelings from this excessive need would leave and I would be at peace.

As I practiced this form of prayer I began to realize that I wasn't praying never to be treated in a special way again. Over that I had no control. I was praying to be free of the *excessive need* to be special. This excessive need is what could render me unloving. What was healed was the unfreedom that leads to a less than loving way of being or a disruption of inner peace. Thus I gradually became free and was at peace whether I was treated specially or not. I became detached from the compulsion.

Becoming aware of an unfreedom, or of a debilitating fear (I have used the prayer in relation to fears as well), is what is key to understanding this prayer. It may be easy for some, difficult for others. As an aid, I have been sharing the following list of obstacles to inner freedom on retreats for some time.

Do I have an excessive need to:

▸ be respected, admired?
▸ be honored, praised?
▸ be preferred to others?
▸ be special?
▸ be consulted?
▸ be included?
▸ be in control?
▸ be ordered?
▸ be perfect?
▸ be thanked?
▸ be always available?
▸ be right all the time?
▸ be always at peace with everybody?
▸ be approved of?
▸ change someone else?

One time, a retreatant gasped upon seeing this list, "Gads, I am all of these!" It is important to take only one excessive need at a time, lest we become emotionally overloaded.

I have successfully applied this form of prayer to a variety of circumstances in my life: to interpersonal relationships, in ministry, to combat fears, and even in situations where there was physical danger.

Being a Jesuit, most of my life has been lived in a community setting. I have shared the following story on retreats. Married couples have told me it clearly speaks to their experience as well.

There was a period in my life when I was especially vulnerable and needed a lot of fraternal support. At the time I was living in a small community in which there was another man who would regularly share with me an account of the various trials he was going through. I have been told that I am a good listener and in fact I do enjoy hearing people's stories. In this case, I would listen in what I thought was a selfless way even though he never asked *me* how I was doing. Eventually, however, I began to feel resentment and was tempted to take revenge: if he was not going to listen to me, then I would stop being there for him.

It so happened that at that time I was reflecting on Thomas Merton's notion of the true self and the false self.[2] An aspect of my true self, I realized, is my ability to enjoy listening to others. But the feeling of resentment and vengefulness was not coming from my true self; this was definitely false self stuff. So, I decided to try the freedom-prayer, but I did so by asking myself a question: *What do I need that this man is not giving me?* I decided to follow this line because I knew some of the problem resided in me. I recalled something the late Anthony de Mello used to say, that other people do not make us unhappy, it's how we react to them. Thus, we need to wake up to the ways we are unfree and realize how much of the emotional pain or suffering we experience is not *caused* by other people, but comes from within ourselves. Perhaps, too, I was following Jesus' admonition, "First take the log out of your own eye, and then you will be able to see clearly to take the speck out of your brother [or sister's] eye" (Matthew 7:5). When I posed the question of what I needed to myself, the answer was: interest. This man seemed to have no interest in hearing my story.

So I applied the freedom-prayer. Every time I felt the spirit of resentment rising, or caught myself in it after the fact, I asked God for freedom from the need for him to be interested in me. Gradually, the feeling of resentment diminished and I was able to be present to the man in a loving way. Eventually, I shared some of this with the man in question, but by then the conversation came from my true self. My being free enabled him to listen without becoming defensive. He is a prayerful person and was also able to grow from the experience.

The freedom-prayer involves a consideration of some of the negative aspects of our personality. This can make us uncomfortable. There is a story in John's gospel that is appropriate here. Jesus was in Jerusalem for a religious festival. He went to the Sheep Gate where there was a pool with five porches. Sick people would gather there in hopes of being healed by the movement of the waters. St. John tells us: A man was there who had been sick for thirty-eight years. Jesus saw him lying there, and he knew that the man had been sick for such a long time; so he asked him, "Do you want to get well?" (5:5-6).

> Do you really want to get well? Do you really
> want to get rid of this excessive need, this
> unfreedom?

> Do you really want to become more loving?

> Are you willing to face the possibility that
> some of the problem between you and anoth-
> er is within yourself?

Jesus' question is a very good question. Until we can
honestly answer yes we will see no reason to pray the
freedom-prayer and thus will remain in that aspect of
our false self, with its disquieting feelings, erroneous-
ly blaming others for our difficulty.

People from various walks of life have written to
tell me how effective the freedom-prayer has been for
them: A high school teacher has found it a great
resource for her classes; counselors and spiritual
directors have shared it with their clients and
directees; people in relationship, whether married or
not, tell me they use it in relation to the other person.
One woman wrote:

> I really like the freedom-prayer. I particular-
> ly find it useful when I react negatively to
> something my husband is doing and even
> though I'm hard pressed at times to express
> exactly what it is I am in need of at that
> moment I just go right ahead and ask God to
> free me from it. I used to worry and fret and
> feel hateful and tight inside. As a result of the
> prayer, I now feel more at ease with myself
> and with my husband.

The most radical account of the success of this
form of prayer that I have heard comes from a woman
in her late forties who told me that when she heard

me give a talk on it she was in a form of depression. She said she had tried to take her life twice. After learning about the prayer, having tried every other avenue of relief she could think of, she composed this version, "God, please free me from the need to take my life." She related that within a month she had not only lost the desire to end her life but had also found a psychiatrist who put her on the proper medication. She told me this two years after she heard the talk.

Encountering Our Fears

Jesus brought a message of freedom: from slavery to the letter of the law, from physical illness for some, from possession for others, from sin as in the case of the paralytic, from humiliation and shame as, for example, for the woman accused of adultery (John 8:1-11), and from fear as when he walked into the locked upper room after his resurrection.

I have also used the freedom-prayer in relation to fears, for those fears that tend to paralyze us. Sometimes I wonder if there isn't a "river of fear" running through me, so often have I used the prayer with this emotion. When I have used the prayer in relation to fears, God has freed me from them too.

Fear is our basic emotion, and some fears can immobilize us. The following is a list of fears that can afflict and freeze us.

▸ the fear of failure
▸ the fear of change
▸ the fear of rejection
▸ the fear of intimacy
▸ the fear of making a mistake
▸ the fear of losing control
▸ the fear of the unknown
▸ the fear of physical injury

▸ the fear of weakness
▸ the fear of freedom

Are you particularly affected by one or more of these fears? Is there another not mentioned here?

Suppose your pastor hears you speaking one day and asks you to be a reader at the Sunday service. One part of you is affirmed by this request, while another is terrified at the thought of reading in public. Try praying for freedom from the fear of making a mistake or from the fear of failure. Or suppose your spouse announces he or she has been offered a job with excellent prospects, but it means moving the family to another part of the country. The idea of leaving what is familiar immobilizes you. Ask God for freedom from the fear of change. Or suppose you have just been to the doctor and received the news that you have cancer and need chemotherapy. Naturally, this news causes a lot of inner turmoil; what side effects the treatment may engender might be one concern. A prayer for freedom from the fear of the unknown can be of help.

If you are having problems in a relationship and have come to realize that they are due to some traumatic experiences as a child, you may have a fear of self-disclosure. Besides getting some counseling to dislodge the psychological blocks within yourself, turn to God in prayer and ask for freedom from the fear of intimacy or from the fear of rejection. What if your prayer is undergoing some profound changes and the word "surrender" keeps coming to mind, but you can't seem to do so. "Lord, please free me from the fear of losing control" is a good antidote. Or suppose you have a feeling that God is inviting you to go to a third-world country to work as a missionary, or to an economically deprived neighborhood in your own country. The idea sounds interesting, but there might be civil or social unrest in the locality and this frightens you into confusion. Ask for freedom from the fear of physical injury.

The fear of freedom needs a bit of interpretation. Michael Cavanagh, in his excellent book *Make Your Tomorrow Better*, explains:

> The fear of freedom is the fear of being bound by significantly less restraints or by no restraints. It is a very subtle fear because most people realize that they fear the imposition of restraints and "naturally" assume that they would welcome its opposite, namely, freedom. But this assumption is invalid for many people. The more freedom we have, the more free rein our impulses have; the more we have to set our own limits; the more we must carve out our own existence; the more we have to assume responsibility for our own behavior. . . .[3]

The fear of freedom entered my life soon after I joined the Jesuits. In the first year of the novitiate, we made a thirty-day retreat on the Spiritual Exercises of St. Ignatius. At the beginning of the retreat, we considered sin and its occurrences in our lives. When I reflected on my own life, the focus of my prayer was on sexuality. I sincerely repented of the mistakes I had made, but as I stated previously, in a desire to be perfect, I went overboard, vowing never to have another woman friend. I shut down my natural, God-given feelings out of fear of going back to my old ways. I entered into what I call a "basement of repression" and remained in this state for six years. Emerging from this inner basement was a cautious and slow process: two steps forward, one back. I found myself praying often for freedom from the fear of making a mistake. However, God patiently led me, particularly through some excellent spiritual guides. It wasn't until ten years after joining the Jesuits, though, that I finally had enough self-confidence to have a woman for a friend. I learned that I could, indeed, set my own limits; that freedom wasn't license; and that being attracted to a woman did not mean I didn't have a vocation to be a priest.

In my prayer, I meditated on Jesus' life and was impressed with the ease with which he related to women. The very fact that there were women in his company (Luke 8:1-3) indicates that he was comfortable in their presence; women trusted him with their problems and their secrets: the Canaanite woman came to him to seek help for her ailing daughter (Matthew 15:21-28); the Samaritan woman at Jacob's well opened her heart to him (John 4:1-42); Mary and Martha, Lazarus' sisters, were his good friends and he often stayed with the family on his way to Jerusalem. In the story of the penitent woman, who washed his feet with perfume and her tears and dried his feet with her hair (Luke 7:36-38), he does not pull away out of fear or embarrassment. He lets her wash his feet and then publicly forgives her sins. He is a model for me of integration, wholeness, and true freedom.

In some of the retreats I have directed older people have shared with me fears that come particularly at this stage of life: the fear of being alone when one's spouse dies, the fear of being abandoned, the fear of becoming dependent on others when one's health begins to decline, the fear of death. I suggested they use the freedom-prayer asking God, in their own words, for the freedom they needed to be free of whatever was upsetting their peace of mind and spirit. Of course, one doesn't have to be in one's later years to experience these fears.

In 1999 I moved from a city to the prairies, from a life mostly lived with other Jesuits in a community setting to living by myself. My closest friends live over an hour away. One of the fears I had to deal with even before the move was the fear of being alone, of being isolated. I recalled St. John's comment that perfect love casts out all fear (1 John 4:18). So, I took my concern to God who is perfect love and who I discerned was inviting me to this situation. And I experienced what the author of Psalm 34 shares: "I prayed to the Lord, and he answered me; he freed me from all my fears" (verse 4). The freeing did not happen immediately. Enough came to get me to my new mission; the rest happened as I learned to adjust to this very different setting. Without God's help, though, I could never have made the transition.

The Steps Involved in the Freedom-Prayer

After practicing the freedom-prayer for about five years, both in relation to excessive needs that led me into unloving behavior and fears that threatened to derail my good intentions, I decided to write down the steps I had been using and the lessons I had learned. I use unfreedom and excessive need interchangeably.

1. I become aware of an unfreedom or of a fear, something that is upsetting my peace of mind and spirit, a way that I find myself acting or feel compelled to act from my false self.

2. I realize I cannot become free of this aspect of my persona through my own efforts; I acknowledge that only God can free me.

3. I believe that God wants to free me, wants me to be more like Jesus, more like Mary, more my true self, because God loves me.

4. I ask God for light to know what it is that I need that I am not receiving (or where I lack freedom). I try to name it. (This is important because it heightens our self-knowledge and humility.)

5. I ask God for freedom from the excessive need I have named, for example, the need to be special, or from the debilitating fear. I pray the phrase, "Lord, please free me from (name the excessive need or fear)," or words to that effect, every time I find myself acting from the unfreedom or the fear or realize later that I have done so.

6. I leave the healing in God's hands, like a child, with complete trust that the freedom will be given to me. I go about life, leaving God to take care of the healing. Therefore, it is not necessary to repeat the prayer often during the day. I say it only at the time I discover I am acting from the unfreedom or fear.

7. What will be healed is the unfreedom, the excessive need, not the thing in itself, for example, the need to be thanked. Thus, I will be at peace whether or not the need is met.

8. Sometimes the freedom prayed for will come right away, at other times it will take awhile. Sometimes God will use the opportunity to free me from more than I asked for, for example, from another aspect of my false self that is connected with the unfreedom that led to the prayer in the first place.

9. It is important not to doubt. If I am of two minds about what I am asking for I can expect nothing to happen (see James 1:5-8 and Mark 11:23).

The Deep Pool

When I share the freedom-prayer on parish missions and retreats, in addition to presenting the nine steps, I also often lead the participants in a guided meditation. In this prayer exercise, one is given the opportunity to get in touch with and let go of an unfreedom, or excessive need, and a paralyzing fear. I am indebted to Fr. Isaias Powers for the basic structure of the meditation; I have adapted it somewhat.[4]

Now that you have had a chance to reflect on some of the unfreedoms and fears listed in this chapter, you may wish to do the following meditation on your own.

In your imagination, be on a hill side.

You have been climbing up this hill because you heard there is a lovely deep pool at the top.

Your climb is made more difficult because you carry two heavy rocks in your coat pockets.

Let the heaviest rock represent an unfreedom, or excessive need, that has kept you bound for many years. Name it.

Let the other rock represent a fear that keeps you from doing what God asks of you. Name the fear.

Feel uncomfortable from the burden of carrying this heaviness . . . as you walk, slowly, painfully uphill until you reach the top.

Now you can see the deep pool.

There is a bridge crossing the pool. Standing at the entrance nearest to you is Mary, Jesus' mother. Imagine what she looks like, what she is wearing.

Walk over and join her beside the bridge and greet her in some way.

Feel her presence. . . .

Take time to be aware of her gentle compassion, her kindly care. . . .

She takes your hand and leads you onto the bridge. She stops at the center of the bridge and looks down into the cool water with you.

In whatever way she wants to tell you, let her convince you to drop those two heavy rocks that you have been carrying into the deep pool. . . .

You may have to struggle with this decision for awhile, for, although, it would be good to be freed of these weights, you might have become so accustomed to living with them, it may be difficult to let them go.

Feel Mary's presence behind you. . . . She puts her hands on your shoulders; you relax at last. Finally, you are able to let the rocks go.

Take each one out of your pockets and drop it into the pool.

Watch them as they drop out of sight. . . . Notice how the rocks muddy the water for awhile. . . . But soon the water settles and the rocks stay down, joining others at the bottom of the pool. . . .

Now, you are free. Experience the feeling of being freed from these burdens.

You are present to God in a new way, available to act and to love as God wishes you to do.

It is time to leave Mary. Thank her for her help and say goodbye to her for now, knowing that you can revisit her whenever you wish.

Make your way off the bridge, to continue your journey.

Now, slowly come back to an awareness of being here in this place.

The figure in the meditation does not always have to be Mary. I have used Jesus at times and once when there were people of the Jewish faith in the audience, I suggested Abraham or Moses.

As we take time to reflect on our unfreedoms, let us remember these words of St. Paul:

Where the Spirit of the Lord is present, there is freedom. All of us, then, reflect the glory of the Lord with uncovered faces; and that same glory, coming from the Lord, who is the Spirit, transforms us into his likeness in an ever greater degree of glory (2 Corinthians 3:17-18).

five

ℐhe Healing Love of ℊod

*Stronger than all the evils
in the soul is the Word,
and the healing power
that dwells in him.*

ORIGEN OF ALEXANDRIA

In her book *Healing Prayer*, Barbara Shlemon shares this touching story.

> One night in 1964 the Lord taught me a lesson about his love which was to change my ideas about suffering and, ultimately, the course of my life. As a professional nurse, I was assigned to the evening shift of a medical-surgical ward in a small Midwest hospital. The report we received from the day shift showed one patient in a comatose condition who would probably expire during the night. The situation was particularly sad because the patient was a young mother of three small children who had put up a valiant fight for life during her stay in the hospital.

As I entered her room to check the flow of her intravenous bottles, I was overcome with sorrow at the sight. The woman's weight had dropped to 90 pounds, most of it concentrated in fluid in her abdomen, which gave her the appearance of a nine-month pregnancy. Her arms and legs were like toothpicks; she had lost all the hair on her body, and jaundice colored her skin a deep yellow. She did not appear to respond to any kind of stimuli, and her breathing was very shallow and irregular.

I glanced at her husband across the room and wished there were words which could convey to him some comfort. The death of his wife seemed very near.

Back at the nurses' station I confessed my feelings of inadequacy to Harriet Saxton, the other nurse on duty with me. She agreed that the situation was grave but she didn't believe it was hopeless. I knew Harriet to be a devout Episcopalian with a deep faith that God really answered prayer. I felt, however, that she was being unrealistic in believing God could or would intervene in this case.

Undaunted by my skepticism, she approached the husband with the suggestion that he contact his parish priest to anoint his wife with the sacrament of extreme unction (now more commonly referred to as the anointing of the sick, a sacrament of healing which can be administered whether or not the person is in danger of death). . . .

The husband took a long while to consider this action and finally decided there was no other recourse. The priest who answered the call was at the hospital within minutes. An elderly man, pastor of the local Catholic church, he quietly read through the Latin ritual, pausing at intervals to apply the holy oil to the sick woman's body. He also brought the holy eucharist with him in the form of a small host, but the woman was in too deep a coma to accept it. The priest gently touched it to her lips and left the hospital.

The whole procedure had only taken minutes, no visible changes had occurred in the patient's condition, and I went off duty that night thinking we had instilled false hope in a hopeless case. The next afternoon found me back on duty. As I walked past the dying woman's room, I glanced in and froze in my tracks. She was sitting up at the side of the bed sipping soup. I couldn't believe it! The day nurse walking past me said, matter-of-factly, "She took a turn for the better last night."[1]

Interest in the healing ministry, in the Catholic church and in some other Christian churches, took a dramatic turn in the late 1960s with the advent of the charismatic renewal. One friend of mine, who has been an active member of this movement for many years, related to me that she experiences God's love in a special way when she is being prayed over by others as they lay their hands on her and when she does this for them. "When I am part of a prayer ministry and I sense the power of God going through my hands to someone I am praying for, I know without a doubt that our God is a loving God."

Sometimes the healing one seeks is not on the physical plane. Friends and retreatants have shared various stories of God's healing love with me. One man experienced the power of God taking violent behavior out of his life and replacing it with gentleness and love, as he relates, "God led me to true manhood, not the illusions I had before of what it is to be a man." Another found healing in a retreat setting: "It was there that I really came face-to-face with who I was, how short I was falling from fulfilling the purpose for which I was created, and that God was inviting me to so much more. I stood before the tabernacle and wept buckets, I really felt God's healing hand for the first time as he gave me his peace."

As Christians, of course, the source of our healing is Jesus Christ who spent a lot of his time in the company of those who were suffering from various kinds of illnesses. The well known theologian, Donald Senior, explains how the gospels portray Jesus as physician and healer.

> *Mark* begins Jesus' ministry with twenty-four hours of nonstop healing in the town of Capernaum (see Mark 1:21-34). Crowds of sick, blind and disabled people cluster around the door of the house where he is staying. Jesus and his disciples cannot even come outside or stop to eat! *Matthew* portrays Jesus as the epic teacher in his Sermon on the Mount, but also as a consummate healer whose compassion and healing power draw crowds of sick and disabled people from every corner of Israel (see Matthew 4:23-25; 15:29-31). In *Luke,* when Jesus gives a kind of inaugural address in the synagogue of Nazareth describing his future ministry, it is very much the "physician" who speaks. His mission, he says, is to "proclaim liberty

to captives and recovery of sight to the blind" (4:18). Jesus then moves out into the countryside of Galilee and Judea to engage in a relentless ministry of healing. And *John* too marks his exalted portrayal of Jesus with great "signs" of healing that show to the world God's redeeming love.[2]

Clearly, Jesus' healing power goes beyond our physical ailments.

Many men and women have experienced deep emotional restoration as well as fortification of will-power through Alcoholics Anonymous. My friend Jack shares a bit of his story: "For many years I had a battle with alcoholism. Through spiritual help from some Carmelite sisters and the AA program and its members, God literally picked me up and carried me until I was strong enough to walk on my own." Cliff credits the healing power of God's love for saving his marriage. He relates:

> I cannot recall any other incident in my life that caused me such pain as the separation of my wife from my life. I recall walking in our garden with our new puppy, praying to God with tears rolling down my cheeks, asking him to inspire my wife to give me just one more chance for forgiveness for my ways. I do not believe I have ever prayed so hard nor felt so helpless. Thanks to God and to our pastor we were able to seek help and get our lives together. Not only was the rift between my wife and I healed but our love for one another deepened.

A friend of mine, who is homosexual, shared how before "coming out of the closet" to a trusted person, he felt lonely and isolated, full of self-hatred. By accepting him as he is, the friend helped heal him at

the very core of his being. He describes the whole
process in terms of conversion.[3]

If the image of God in us is to reach its full potential, we need to face those aspects of our lives that are
not healthy, be they in the emotional, social, or spiritual realms. This means facing our weaknesses. A
wonderful prayer exercise to facilitate this kind of
inner healing is called *Emmaus Walk*.[4]

> When you find strong negative feelings per-
> sisting in your experience, you need to go on
> an Emmaus walk with Jesus.
>
> First, quiet yourself and enter the presence of
> One who walks with you as a friend. Jesus
> asks you to share with him what is troubling
> you. He wants to share your passion just as
> you share his.
>
> Next, tell him about the way you see what is
> happening to you and how you feel; whatev-
> er is troubling you, however you feel you
> need to be healed.
>
> Ask him how he feels about you. Let him
> accept you where you are. Let him remind
> you that he is familiar with all your weak-
> nesses as he experienced weakness himself.
> He says, "I know exactly how you feel, for I
> have been down that road myself."
>
> Now let Jesus tell you some of the things he
> appreciates about you, especially in that area
> of your life where you now find yourself
> most vulnerable. Let him tell you that he
> loves you most where you love yourself
> least.

Finally, thank him in some way for his wholehearted, healing, acceptance of you. And, be at peace.

Edward Ingebretsen has written a poem that poignantly describes this inner search for wholeness. It's called "Diving Into the Wreck."

Diving into the wreck
as the poet says—
so the digging goes on
in the basements of my heart.

Is it a well
or a mine?
Down is the direction
either way.

Shall water flow
or coal shine?
The chemistry
only confuses me.

Dig me deep.
Dig through the shallows
and blinds
to the God
who is in me
like a small steel heart
or an endless stomach
keeping me hungry.

Dig me deep.
Lord of brokenness
I shall have nothing else—
rich as I am still
in this:
my major vacancy.[5]

In her insightful book on the Easter mysteries, Beatrice Bruteau connects God's healing power to what happened to Jesus immediately after his death. Reflecting on our need, at times, to be healed of the root causes of our woundedness, she writes:

> You have to go down to the root and relieve whatever is wrong there. This is why Jesus is represented as going down into hell to set the prisoners free. . . . The spirits in prison are the consciousness-energies in us, our spiritual powers shackled by fear and pain and therefore unable to move in accord with the true generosity of the real self. . . . My suggestion is that it is only when these imprisoned powers hear the Good News— the truth of God's love and of their own belonging to divine life—that the bonds fall away. . . . All our guilts and fears and hatreds and griefs and refusals to love, our memories of hurt, our repressed feelings, whatever we have in our hell-prison, the Christ-Spirit heals and releases.[6]

We need courage to invite Jesus to descend into our depths, there to remove the scars from our injured self.

Have you experienced this kind of in-depth healing in your life? If so, in what aspect of your being: the physical, emotional, mental, and/or spiritual? Is there anything you feel you need to bring to the Lord for healing now, any way in which you want to invite him to descend into a wounded part of yourself?

I came across the following prayer (author unknown) while preparing to give a retreat. It expresses well the sentiments of the wounded heart.

Jesus, I come now before you, in the weakness that has overcome me, with the feelings that I find difficult to share and try to hide, with the emptiness that sometimes grips me, and with the resentments that can paralyze me. I come in faith and trust, in humility and reverence, and I ask to be *relieved* and *healed*.

You took human weakness on yourself when you lived as a human being, suffered and died for my sake. By rising from the dead, you manifested your victory over all forms of death. Because of this my trust in you is firm. I believe you can overcome the negative feelings I experience, the troublesome thoughts that plague me, the wounded memories that haunt me.

Look upon me with your healing compassion and love. I ask this for my own peace of mind and spirit and for the sake of those whose lives I touch. Amen.

By means of poetry Daniel Berrigan prays in a similar vein:

At land's end, end of tether
where the sea turns in sleep
ponderous, menacing
and my spirit fails and runs
landward, seaward, askelter

I pray you
make new
this hireling heart

O
turn your face to me
—winged, majestic, angelic—
tireless,

a tide
my prayer goes up—
show me your face, O God![7]

The Healing Mission of Jesus

After Jesus chose the twelve apostles, St. Luke tells
us he came down a hill to a level place (6:12-19). A
large crowd had gathered to hear him. Many were in
search of healing as well: "All the people tried to
touch him, for power was going out from him and
healing them all" (6:19). What might some contemporary examples of this healing ministry be?

Al has been in elementary school education for
twenty-one years, the last eleven as a principal. He
shares his vision:

> Over the years I have encountered many dif-
> ferent students, parents, and families, each
> with their own issues and concerns. I have
> seen many of those I have worked with in
> my vocation as a Catholic educator with
> their own pain and brokenness. I see Christ
> in students and parents, particularly the suf-
> fering Christ when I see the pain in their
> lives. That Christ is calling out for tenderness
> and compassion, for understanding and for-
> giveness, for acceptance and support. I can
> only but respond accordingly because if I do
> not then I have been less than honest with
> myself. Being a teacher and a principal are
> the most important things I have done with
> my life; they have helped me to see God in
> others. I experience God reaching out and
> touching, with compassion and healing,
> those who walk into the doors of my school.

When I was in my late twenties, I went to counseling for a year and a half. I had suffered a brief encounter with depression and discovered, through the insights of the therapist, that the cause of the depressing feelings was a repression of anger. Growing up in a strong, patriarchal family had not encouraged, it seemed, the expression of angry feelings. I thank God for leading me to this particular counselor, for he used his therapeutic gifts for healing with patience and understanding. In addition, he supported my connecting the counseling process with my prayer life. Consequently, I experienced the healing presence of Jesus throughout the year and a half. In the next chapter I will share a significant healing episode from my recent journey that has had profound ramifications on my life.

Significant healing goes on in society as well. We can see Jesus' healing hand when ethnic groups come together in reconciliation, when legislation is passed that ensures the rights of our most impoverished citizens, when the general public respond generously to a community or a country in crisis. People like Dorothy Day, Cesar Chavez, Edwina Gateley, and Jean Vanier exercise the healing power of Jesus in such a way that all of us are affected by their actions.[8]

The Other Side of God's Healing Love

What happens to our faith when what we pray to be healed of, sometimes pleading to God in a desperate way, isn't taken away? Do we begin to doubt the love and compassion of God? There is certainly that temptation. Or, is there something else God wishes to teach us in these situations?

In the fall of 1997 I drove from San Diego, California, to Calgary, Alberta, a four day journey. I went to give some parish missions and retreats in the

Calgary Diocese and stayed for three months. About ten days before I was to drive home, I dislocated something in my upper back while moving a box of books. At the time, though, I thought I had simply pulled a muscle. And so, after a quick trip to a chiropractor, I headed back to the United States and San Diego in my car. By the time I arrived home, both sides of my upper back were sore. I had a month to see about the injury before returning to Canada for another two months. No significant damage could be ascertained by my doctor so, with muscle relaxant pills in hand, I headed north in the car again, this time going by a different route and with frequent stops along the way. On the trip I managed to get a couple of soothing massages and availed myself of Jacuzzis at two friends' homes where I stayed en route.

I arrived in Calgary a week before the first parish mission. A hip problem I have had for years flared up. This, combined with my back which was still sore, interrupted my sleeping. I was at my wits end. I was tempted to discouragement. And then I read in the newspaper about a Kenyan cross-country athlete who had fallen during his race at the Winter Olympics. Although he came in last, the winner embraced him and called him a true champion. When asked about the race he replied, "I thought about quitting, but I had come too far to quit, so I picked myself up and kept going." This was an inspiration for me, so far from home as well. It gave me renewed courage as I prepared for the parish mission.

I had been begging God to heal me of my physical problem so I could do his work. Instead, I began to realize I had been receiving all kinds of help to carry this cross. As Lent was about to begin, I started to rethink my prayer for a complete healing, especially of the back problem, right now. I came up with a new prayer, for interior conversion, so that I would be at peace whether or not I was healed. I asked God to help me stop worrying about how long ago the injury happened since those kinds of thoughts always ended up in fear and anxiety. I asked for the grace to simply live one day at a time.

At the first parish mission, the pastor introduced me to the congregation at each Sunday Mass. Just before the first Mass, while I was sitting in the church praying, I happened to look up at the first Station of the Cross. Jesus stood alone in the painting, the crown of thorns upon his head, but what really caught my attention were ropes that surrounded his back; ropes in exactly the same place as my pain was! I felt God was affirming my acceptance prayer of a few days before. I sensed Jesus inviting me to carry my cross in union with him and to offer up any discomfort I was experiencing for the parishioners. I determined to put my trust in him to give me the inner strength I needed to persevere in this undertaking.

The commitment I made to carry this cross has had its ups and downs, as the difficulty with my back continues. Sometimes I have been encouraged by a reading at daily Mass, such as, "Be strong in the Lord and in the strength of his power" (Ephesians 6:10 NRSV).

A friend shared a quote from Eleanor Roosevelt that gave me extra motivation when I wasn't feeling quite up to doing some ministry: "You must do the things you think you cannot do." Cardinal Carlo Martini's profound reflections on Job in his book *Perseverance in Trials* has been a major aid whenever I am in a "down time." In his "Introduction to the Mystery of Trials" chapter, after suggesting that the attitude we should foster when faced with a difficult cross is acceptance, he introduces the concept of the "risk of reflection." He explains:

With the help of God's grace, human beings can quickly adopt an attitude of submission. Immediately thereafter, however, comes the time of reflection, which is the worst trial of all. The Book of Job might have ended at the end of the second chapter, after showing that Job stood fast because his love of God was real and genuine. In fact, however, we must wait and see, for the situation of Job is not that of a human being who is content to sigh and accept his lot once and for all. Rather it is the concrete situation of a human being who having once expressed acceptance must embody that acceptance day after day.

We ourselves have a similar experience at times: when faced with a difficult decision or a momentous event, we are swept along by the enthusiasm and courage that are given to us in life's hard moments. But a little reflection then opens the door to turmoil of mind, and we experience the difficulty of accepting that to which we gave our assent. . . . The difficulty is to persevere in this assent for a lifetime and under the pressure of feelings and mental conflict.[9]

Is there anything in your life that has not been healed despite your prayer?

What has been your attitude about this?

Have you learned anything during this struggle?

After I returned to the United States from Canada, God gave me contact with two extraordinary people who fully embody "persevering for a lifetime" their assent to physical difficulties. They are Father Gregory Tolaas and Mary Ann Shields. Both are in their mid-forties. Each, in their own way, has had a profound effect on my life and on many others as well. Father Tolaas, who has had a daily struggle with the fatal disease cystic fibrosis since he was born, is pastor of an inner city parish in the Midwest. He was interviewed in an issue of *Praying* magazine. I would like to share some excerpts from that interview.[10] He begins by talking about the severity of his illness.

> Cystic fibrosis in my case tends to be a real aggressor. Each morning I wake up feeling very congested and very tight and trapped in my chest. I am aware that throughout the day I need to do hours of therapy and aerosols and pounding treatments and some aerobic activity to keep my lungs working, to try to outrun the disease. . . . With CF, I've needed to realize that the race is pretty constant and that life is uphill. I don't get any downhill days. That demands a certain psychological adjustment and a certain spiritual evolution or cultivation inside of one's heart to say, how do I view my life and how do I do my life if each day is a working day and not a weekend day when you have time off.

In response to a question by the interviewer, Father Tolaas reflects on the emotional struggles he has been through in relation to the disease.

> At times I am visited by deep discouragement, by deep anger with my disease. . . . Sometimes I really hit the wall, and I can be enraged by it. . . . I have needed to learn to recognize and name and own my anger and my tears.

When faced with the reality that despite his deep desire for an eradication of the illness, it did not go away, he reflects on the spiritual dimensions of his life.

I realized, life has storms, it has valleys of great darkness and tribulations at times, and you can either do life without God or do life with God. . . . I came to see that God is the One who crawls into the bed with the one who is suffering and suffers with and walks with and dies with and rises with. . . . If the incarnation of Jesus means Emmanuel, God with us, *sometimes God with us is what we get and is enough, which is different from God fixing us or answering every physical need* [emphasis mine].

Now, years later, he has come to a startling conclusion about his sickness:

I don't know that it would be to my greatest benefit to be healed, because the CF has kept me very close to God, it has kept me very aware of my dependence upon something bigger than myself, to sustain me, to walk with me and to help me do my life. . . . For me, the relationship I have with God, woven into the stuff of my story, it's pretty embedded. I don't think anybody could convince me God doesn't exist or God doesn't love me or walk with me in my life.

I came across the interview of Father Tolaas just as it was beginning to dawn on me that I might have this weakness in my back for the rest of my life. In fact, not long before, I had been led to pray for the gift of patience and long-suffering in all the events of life. When I read his reflection on the word Emmanuel, "sometimes God with us is what we get and is enough," I felt a deep resonance. No matter how many times I had asked God to heal me, no matter how many holy-healers had prayed over me, the problem persisted. God had not abandoned me, though. He kept reminding me of his loving presence by the numerous helps I received to carry my cross, which brings me to the second extraordinary person.

I met Mary Ann Shields at her wedding. That very week, I was in a down time, a desert, as my back had been acting up. In fact, I stopped at the chiropractor on the way to the church. I had been invited to this celebration by Mary Ann's fiancé, Denny, who had participated in a men's retreat I had given. Denny greeted me warmly when I arrived. I told him I'd like to meet his bride before the service. He pointed me to the place where she and her parents were waiting. I walked over and as I came near to them I noticed she was in a wheelchair. My first thought was, "it must have been a water skiing accident," as it was summer time. But when I got close enough to introduce myself, I could see Mary Ann was paralyzed. Seeing her like this hit me like a ton of bricks!

I had received relief for my problem by stopping for an adjustment on the way to the wedding, but it was obvious she did not have that option. Suddenly, my physical ailment seemed to shrink in importance. There was more to come.

The pastor explained to me there would be six priests concelebrating the nuptial Mass. He showed me the seating area for the clergy and asked me to choose one of two seats in the second row. Since the other five priests knew the couple well, I chose the seat furthest from the altar. This put me next to the musicians. After we took our places, I turned to greet the closest musician to me. It was the cantor. I was stunned to see that she, too, was in a wheelchair, also

paralyzed! I felt as if God had thrown two huge bar-
rels of ice water in my face! Mary Ann had been shock
enough, but here were *two* people who had, obvious-
ly, come to grips with their disability and were func-
tioning quite well. These two women inspired me to
pray for a higher threshold for pain and discomfort
for myself.

Since the wedding, a friendship has developed
between Denny and Mary Ann and myself. I learned
that she has an M.B.A., was at that time chief financial
officer for a construction company, and is highly
regarded in the county where she lives as a consultant
on money matters. One evening she shared that she
has been in a wheelchair since she was six years old,
as the result of a virus. I asked her to write down
some of her reflections, which follow.

> As a child, my parents always encouraged
> me to pray for miracles, especially for the
> miracle of being able to walk again.
> Sometime after my paralysis set in, my
> mother began driving me thirty miles every
> Thursday morning to an Episcopal church
> prayer meeting. I distinctly remember one
> Thursday when the priest laid hands on my
> head and everyone prayed for me.
>
> The priest promised me that God would take
> good care of me and heal me so that I could
> walk again. I had an overwhelming sense of
> comfort, warmth, and peace. It was as if I
> could feel God flowing through my head
> down to my toes. Somehow I knew that God
> would always take care of me.
>
> It wasn't until I was a teenager that I realized
> that perhaps I would never be able to walk
> again. But I knew that the world held so

many opportunities whether I did them as a walking person or did them from a wheelchair.

As a young adult, there was an instance when I experienced God's love in an absolute way. I don't know whether I was dreaming or not, but I heard God say to me, "Look, Mary Ann, out of all of the six-year-old children in the world, I chose you to live the rest of your life from a chair."

My understanding from this was that God had personally selected me to serve him, to be an example of his love and to teach others through living a faith-filled life.

It seemed to me that what God wanted me to convey to others was much more powerful coming from me in a wheelchair than it would have been as a walking person, and that I now had a personal *responsibility* to do this for the glory of God.

What a truly remarkable person! What is amazing is how deeply her greatness of heart has impacted me. If I had not been in my wilderness, or desert experience, brought on by the back injury, I would not have been so affected; I know that. Eugene Peterson, in his excellent book *Leap Over a Wall: Reflections on the Life of David*, points out that in our wilderness times, our perceptions begin to sharpen—sights, sounds, smells.[11] Our awareness of God's presence deepens if we are open to it. We meet the God of surprises. However, we need to let go of whatever security we have been hanging onto: for me, it was the idol of perfect health and the severe dislike of pain, of discomfort, of inconvenience. If we can even let go of our need for physical healing, as Gregory Tolaas, Mary Ann, and many others have done, preferring instead "Thy Will be done," we can be at peace as we are. That is a gift beyond price. That is a healing miracle.

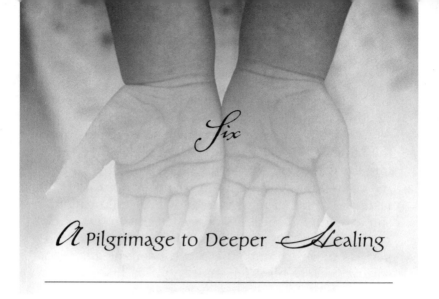

Six

A Pilgrimage to Deeper *Healing*

The Lord heals the broken-hearted
and bandages their wounds.

PSALM 147:3

Occasionally, God leads us on a healing journey that takes us back to our childhood. This happened to me in 1995-1996 when I first began giving parish missions and retreats in southern Alberta. The following is an account of the process I went through which turned out to be essential to my eventual move from the United States.[1]

Before I tell the story, I want to introduce the idea of the "vision quest" since it plays a part in the way I understand these events.

The vision quest, a ritual that still survives among some Native American peoples, is designed to facilitate a boy's entrance into manhood. The time of his first vision quest takes place as puberty begins. To fulfill his responsibilities as a future hunter and warrior, the boy needs a guardian spirit. However, to discover this spirit, it is necessary for the boy to fast. His body, depleted by the lack of food, becomes receptive to the spirits within the natural world. These spirits appear in visions during dreamlike trances.

When a boy or his father believes the time is ripe, the father takes his son away from their village and into the woods. There they build a simple structure in which the boy will live for as many as four days of fasting. The father returns to the village, allowing his son to begin his quest. As hunger begins to set in, the boy sits and waits, occasionally falling into unsettled periods of sleep, until the eagerly sought guardian spirit comes to him. This spirit will be his personal guide and protector on his life journey. Sometimes the spirit bestows special gifts on the boy—for example, the power to heal or to conduct tribal ceremonies. Continued direct contact between the boy and his guardian spirit will periodically be renewed by further vision quests.

The key elements in a vision quest are: allowing oneself to be led apart from what is one's ordinary (or "safe") place, fasting, listening with one's heart for the voice of the guardian spirit, returning to the community to share the gift(s) received, and staying open and ready for future vision quests.

When I look back on my own life, I think my first vision quest occurred when I realized I had a vocation to religious life. The "woods" for me was the Jesuit novitiate. It was there, while on a thirty-day silent retreat, that the idea to be a Jesuit priest was clearly confirmed in my prayer by the Holy Spirit. That was thirty-eight years ago. Since then I have felt God's inviting presence in my life in a number of ways.

Was there a special experience in your life, whether you are a man or a woman, that fits the description of the vision quest?

As profound as that early experience of transformation was for me, I want to focus here on what I call my midlife vision quest. This enterprise extended, much to my surprise, for more than a year.

New Adventure Raises Fears

My story begins in the fall of 1995, when I traveled to the diocese of Calgary to give two parish missions. I was excited at the prospect of a new adventure and the response from the parishioners at each of the churches was overwhelming—they were so open and enthusiastic. However, I did not realize how deeply I had been affected by the faith of those people until I returned to San Diego. I experienced in my prayer an invitation from the Spirit to change the direction that had characterized my life since 1986. After the summer of that year, I had spent every even-numbered summer giving retreats in Ireland. There I had found a second home. Now I was being asked to go to Calgary instead.

During my trip to give the parish missions, I learned of the shortage of priests there and how some priests had experienced difficulty in getting a replacement so they could go on vacation. I volunteered to fill in for three pastors over a two-month period and was promptly booked.

A few months before I was to depart the fears started to surface. I was to spend the month of June in a country parish about twenty miles west of Calgary where I had given a mission. Saint Mary's Church and rectory stand on a hill overlooking the peaceful town of Cochrane. There are no neighbors close by, and I would be by myself. In addition, the closest Jesuit community to Calgary is over five hundred miles away. One day it dawned on me that I had a fear of living alone. I searched my memory for the cause of this fear and vaguely connected it with a house I had lived in as a child. What happened in the house was that by the age of thirteen, my parents would leave me in charge of my two baby sisters, ages six and four, when they needed an evening out. It was a two-story house with a lot of rooms and I was afraid to be in it alone after dark. I realize now that I have dreaded those evenings my parents would leave me in charge. The combination of these two realities disturbed me. No matter where I have traveled, I have lived in the company of others, and always with easy access to other Jesuits. Now I faced living on my own, outside my own country and culture. I was being led apart from what had become secure; I was being led into the "woods" again.

My stay in Cochrane was filled with many blessings. As I faced my fear of living alone by actually doing it, God often spoke to me in the entrance antiphons at daily mass. Frequently there were passages about relying on God's strength and power. I felt empowered by God's sustaining love.

The pastor had given me a lovely book by Barry Lopez as a gift. Called *Crow and Weasel*, it is a story about two Indian braves who travel farther north than any of their people have ever gone. One day on their journey they come upon a stranger. After Crow explains why he and Weasel are traveling, the stranger says: "I am going to the West. I am on a vision quest. I am traveling a long way myself. Among my people, west is the direction we fear most, so that is the direction we travel when we go on a vision quest."[2] The timing of my reading this, in the middle of June, startled me into greater courage and commitment to facing my own fears.

As I fasted from Jesuit contact, new community gradually formed in the faces and hearts of the parishioners. I gradually came to realize that I had two goals for the summer: to draw closer in union with God and to come nearer to my own inner truth.

During Lent, when I discovered my fears of living alone, I had prayed that Jesus would descend into my own inner darkness, just as he had descended into darkness after his resurrection (as we pray in the Apostles' Creed). I asked him to free me from whatever fears I had about living alone and to heal me of the root cause of those fears. I faced the fear of living alone in Cochrane. It was during my time in the next parish that the healing of the root cause was initiated. My vision quest, it turned out, was not yet finished.

Unexpected Insights

Fortunately, I had planned to take a week's holiday after leaving the parish in Cochrane. Southern Alberta is so beautiful, and I wanted to experience some of its grandeur. I also looked forward to attending the Calgary Stampede. Thus it was that I arrived at the second parish rested and refreshed.

Instead of staying in the rectory of my next assignment, I accepted an invitation from a family of the parish to housesit for them while they went on vacation. I had met them the previous October. Soon after I moved in, memories of the house I had lived in as a child came flooding into my consciousness. It turned out that some of the characteristics of the family for whom I was housesitting were similar to those of my own family. This family included four teenagers: three boys and a girl. I stayed in one of the boys' rooms. As I slowly came to the realization that God was purifying me of something from my past, I was amazed, because I did not know that there was anything from that time of my life that needed healing. By the end of my stay in that house, I felt a sense of peace. However, any hope that I had finally come to the end of my inner pilgrimage was dashed a month later during my annual eight-day retreat, which I made back in California.

California Dreaming

I spent my retreat reading and reflecting on my journal from the summer. My prayer progressed smoothly for the first six days as I recalled events and graces, times I had experienced God's strengthening and sustaining love, fears faced and overcome. It was on the seventh day that I considered the house I had lived in while the family was on vacation. During one of the prayer periods, something seemed to erupt within me. Whatever it was, the sensation scared me, and I decided to cease reflecting on the house for a while. I was about to go on vacation and wanted to enjoy it.

One day during my vacation I went to a bookstore and picked up a copy of Robert Johnson's book *Inner Work*. I had read some of his other books, and the title of this one appealed to me. However, I did not begin reading it until I was back at work ten days later.

It was in the first section of Johnson's book, "Waking Up to the Unconscious," that the Spirit started speaking to me. I read:

> The idea of the unconscious derives from a simple observation in daily human life: There is material contained in our minds that we are not aware of most of the time. We sometimes become aware of a memory, a pleasant association, an ideal, a belief that wells up unexpectedly from an unknown place . . . a sudden invasion of energy from the unconscious. . . . These hidden parts of ourselves have strong feelings and want to express them.[3]

Suddenly, I realized what I had experienced on the seventh day of my retreat: an eruption from my unconscious. Johnson continues as follows:

> Unless we learn to do inner work, these parts of ourselves are hidden from our conscious view. . . . The incorporation of unconscious materials must continue until, finally, the conscious mind reflects the wholeness of the total self.[4]

I was greatly relieved by these words and realized that I had nothing to fear from the experience I had while on retreat. I now understood what had happened. I could safely continue doing the necessary inner work on this pilgrimage of deeper healing. I chose the following prayer to help me face whatever was coming: "Loving God, lead me to seek beyond my reach and give me the courage to stand before your truth."

On October 9, almost a year to the day since I had felt the Spirit call me to Canada instead of Ireland for the summer, I had a significant dream. There were only men in this dream. I (the dream ego) had on a bright plaid shirt, others were dressed in gray. One man was completely different from the others: disheveled and scruffy-looking, he had a bandage on the side of his head. He shied away from me whenever I tried to make contact with him.

When I awakened, I immediately wrote down an account of the dream, intending to do the dream work as soon as I had time. However before I had a chance to do it, my reflections took me to the house I had lived in as a child (I call it "the house on Doresta Road").

It needs to be pointed out here that sections of Johnson's book are on dream analysis and active imagination. I have been working on my dreams for many years, so in part this was a refresher course. However, this was the first time I had heard of active imagination. The main purpose of this inner-work technique is to provide communication from the conscious self to those elements of the unconscious that one may be cut off from or that may be in need of healing. One does this by using the language of images, entering into a dialogue with them. One goes to the unconscious through the imagination and invites an image to come forth. Then one writes down the dialogue that occurs: what the conscious self says, what the interior "persons" reply, and what they do together. Johnson cautions anyone attempting to use this tool for inner understanding to have someone available to visit or phone in case they become overwhelmed by the imagination and cannot turn it off.

Following on my dream and the memory of my childhood house, I decided to invite my inner child to come forth. There seemed to be a connection between the injured man and this child. In terms of the vision quest, I was listening to the voice of my guardian spirit who, I felt, was leading me in this direction.

Revisiting Doresta Road

I was eight years old when my family moved to the house on Doresta Road. It was our second major move in two years, which is traumatic enough for a child of that age. As I reflected on this, two images came to mind: a lush, green meadow and the house. The meadow was a place of innocence, joy, and playfulness. A little boy was there, as well as a shepherd, and myself as an adult. There was a lot of positive energy in the meadow. Light characterized this serene place. It soon became clear to me that whenever I felt overwhelmed by the second image, the house, I could go to the meadow for relief—a remedy I was to use more than once, as it turned out, since the mood of the house on Doresta Road, when I imagined it, was somber, serious, fearful, dark. Difficult to be playful here, I thought.

I invited the little boy to come to my consciousness, assuring him that I would not harm him, that I wanted only to help him. We gradually got acquainted, and then he asked me if I would go into the house with him. I suggested we bring the shepherd too (who by then had become a Christ figure for me). The boy agreed. And so the three of us entered the house through the front door. I held the child's hand. As we walked from room to room an amazing thing happened. Each room, and each part of it, became bathed in light. The mood in each room turned from somber to serene. Whenever the mood got too heavy as we entered a room, I would switch to the meadow. Sometimes I would stop the process altogether and take a walk or watch something mindless on television.

It took two days to cover the entire house on Doresta Road, as it had a lot of rooms. We even walked through the back and front yards. By the time we finished, the house and the entire grounds were covered in light. Even the boy and I were bathed in light. I felt as if a miracle had happened in my psyche. God had healed me of a part of my past that I did not even know was in need of restoration. It was pure gift.

At the time I did the active imagination, I was in close proximity to a Jesuit friend of mine who is knowledgeable in the ways of the mind and the heart. I went to see him after I had finished the inner work. He listened attentively to my story and gave me some excellent feedback. He recognized that some serious, though not devastating, injury to my self-esteem had occurred in the house on Doresta Road. He suggested that the transformation of the house from dark to light may permit me further access to a deeper level of meaning. He also suggested doing another dialogue with the little boy to see how he was feeling now. And, because I told my Jesuit friend about the dream with the man who had a bandage on his head, he further encouraged me to enter into a dialogue with him. This would mean combining active imagination with dream analysis to complete the healing process. Lastly he suggested that I ritualize the healing somehow as a way of celebrating what had occurred.

As I entered into what was to be the final part of my year-long transformation, I took courage from Psalm 18: "I love you, O Lord, my strength, O Lord, my rock, my fortress, my deliverer. My God, my rock of refuge, my shield, my saving, my stronghold!" (NAB). I found that I still needed God's grace to carry out my Jesuit friend's suggestions. Even though the house on Doresta Road was now bathed in light, I wasn't sure where the search for deeper meaning would take me.

Stunning Revelation

One day during my prayer, a couple of weeks after I had visited my Jesuit friend, I entered into a dialogue with God about the house on Doresta Road. I asked God if he wanted to take me to another level of meaning about our family home. What transpired then was a shocking revelation to me. I heard God saying, "I was there too, with you and your family even though you did not know me. My love has always been with you. Through your infant years, in the time you lived on Doresta Road, as a teenager, I have always been there."

This was the deeper meaning of the house! I was stunned, not having realized this before. It was a spiritual bombshell for me. Knowing that God had been there through all my times of turmoil, during the normal ups and downs of life, the joys and hurts of my childhood, my successes and failures, was a source of great happiness and peace.

Were there particular hurts associated with the house that needed healing?

Now it was time to revisit the boy, my inner child. I called him forth from my unconscious. He emerged willingly. I asked him how he was. He responded, "I am fine. I feel so much better since we went into the house with the shepherd. Not only is the house bathed in light, but I am too. Thank you for taking me there with you. I am no longer afraid. I feel safe."

By now, I had realized the connection between the little boy and the man with the bandaged head. Both represented parts of me. The disheveled, dirty, scruffy-looking, timid adult had been injured as a child. He represented a part of me that was still wounded. It was time to call him forth from the dream I had written down over a month before. I asked him if we could talk. "How are you feeling?" I inquired.

No longer shy in my presence, he answered, "I am much better now that you have taken the time to see to my wound. I thought you had forgotten me and didn't care about me. Now I feel wanted and secure. My head has healed. I have taken off the bandage. I have bathed and have a new set of clothes. I feel good about myself." I told him I was sorry he had had to suffer for so long, but that I had not known of his existence until he had surfaced in the dream. I thanked him for appearing to me, letting me know of his distress. Then I asked if there was anything else I could do for him. "Yes," he responded. "Please give me a hug." Then he added, "And your blessing." And so I did both, thus bringing to conclusion a remarkable year of grace.

I now come to the fourth key element of a vision quest: returning to the community to share the gift received. This I have endeavored to do honestly and openly. I hope what I have learned and experienced will be a help to you, reader, as you continue on your journey.

My prayer is that you and I will both always remain open and ready for whatever our loving God has in store for us, for whatever vision quests are still waiting out there. We wait in hope, relying on God's strength.

Seven

The Protective Love of *God*

When you pass through deep waters, I will be
    with you;
your troubles will not overwhelm you.
When you pass through fire,
you will not be burned;
the hard trials that come will not hurt you.

Isaiah 43:2

One of the earliest accounts of God's protective love
in the New Testament happens at the very beginning
of Jesus' life. Mary and Joseph had planned to return
to their home in Nazareth after their part in the cen-
sus was completed and Mary was strong enough to
travel. However, fate intervened in the violent and
jealous nature of King Herod. Joseph, no stranger to
receiving messages in his dreams, is given a warning
in one. An angel of the Lord appears to him and says:
"Herod will be looking for the child in order to kill
him. So get up, take the child and his mother and
escape to Egypt, and stay there until I tell you to
leave" (Matthew 2:13).

In the Old Testament, especially through the prophets and the book of Psalms, there are a wide variety of images that convey the protective love of God: God is a rock, a shield, a fortress, a strong city; God is our refuge and our strength; the dark valley will not be a source of harm because God is with us; the right hand of the Lord, a symbol of strength, sustains us; God guards his vineyard; we need not fear the terror of the night; God rescues us from the fowler's snare. One of the clearest descriptions of this aspect of God's love is found in Psalm 91:

> Whoever goes to the Lord for safety,
> whoever remains under the protection of the
>   Almighty,
> can say to him,
> "You are my defender and protector.
> You are my God; in you I trust."
> He will keep you safe from all hidden dangers
> and from all deadly diseases.
> He will cover you with his wings;
> you will be safe in his care;
> his faithfulness will protect and defend you.
> You need not fear any dangers at night
> or sudden attacks during the day
> or the plagues that strike in the dark
> or the evils that kill in daylight. . . .
> God will put his angels in charge of you
> to protect you wherever you go
>   (Psalm 91:1-6, 11).

The image of the eagle not only expresses God's providence as we saw earlier, but also God's protection. The passage from Deuteronomy is worth considering again here. "Like an eagle teaching its young to fly, catching them safely on its spreading wings, the Lord kept Israel from falling" (32:11). The eagle is a powerful symbol in North American aboriginal spirituality as well. It represents courage, strength, guidance, and freedom. Because the eagle flies higher than any living creature, it is respected as closest to the face of God. With its sharp vision and powerful wings, it is a profound image of the protective love of God.[1] Those who trust in this characteristic of God's love will find renewed strength, the prophet Isaiah tells us, "They will rise on wings like eagles; they will run and not get weary; they will walk and not grow weak" (40:31).

Human fear is overcome by trust in the protective love of God. A scripture professor once told me that the most often used phrase in the entire Bible is a variation of "you need not fear." Both Mary and Joseph are encouraged not to be afraid when the announcements of Jesus' birth comes to them. Many people in the Bible, from Moses, to the prophets, to Mary and Joseph, to the apostles are urged to put away their fear.

Joshua, the successor to Moses received this divine message: "Remember that I have commanded you to be determined and confident! Do not be afraid or discouraged, for I, the Lord your God, am with you wherever you go" (Joshua 1:9).

One of the most personal of Old Testament passages can be appreciated even more if you substitute your name for "Israel." It is from the prophet Isaiah: "Israel, the Lord who created you says, 'Do not be afraid—I will save you. I have called you by name—you are mine'" (43:1).

Nowhere in the New Testament is the encouragement to put aside one's fear more clearly stated then on a certain night on the Lake of Galilee. The apostles were quite a ways from shore when a strong wind came up. St. John explains:

> The disciples had rowed about three or four
> miles when they saw Jesus walking on the

water, coming near the boat, and they were terrified. "Don't be afraid," Jesus told them, "it is I." Then they willingly took him into the boat, and immediately the boat reached land at the place they were heading for (6:19-21).

Whether the setting is the wilderness, a barren desert, a storm, or a dark wood at night, the message is the same: put your trust in God, be not afraid.[2] We need only recall the Israelites' early experiences with God to know this is true: "[God] found them wandering through the desert, a desolate, wind-swept wilderness. He protected them and cared for them, as he would protect himself" (Deuteronomy 32:10). Even in our old age, God continues to care for our welfare (Isaiah 46:4).

Be Not Afraid

I have been on a steady diet of God's protective love for a long time. My first recollection of this dimension of the love of God, as a Jesuit, goes back to a time before I was ordained. It was in the mid-1960s. I was living and working in an inner city African-American parish in San Francisco. There was a lot of racial tension in those days. One day I was walking down the main street of the neighborhood. Ahead of me, five or six young African-American men were leaning against a wall. I did not know any of them. Clerical collar or not, they stared at me with what I perceived as hatred and distrust as I approached them. I was afraid. From somewhere inside of me came an unexpected overture; I smiled at them and greeted them in a friendly tone. Their response was equally unexpected; my manner seemed to disarm them and they responded in a friendly way. As I continued on my way, the words "he went straight through their midst and walked away" came to mind (Luke 4:28-30).

In 1980, I began a ministry of giving workshops and retreats. Up to that time I was on a school calendar schedule, with regular time off for holidays and vacation. However, this new ministry didn't have any such boundaries. I started getting invitations to lead a retreat right in the middle of what used to be time for rest. In addition, I took engagements back to back with hardly a break in between. When I started getting headaches, I knew I had to do something to change the rhythm of my life. Then, a curious phenomenon began happening in my dreams: African-American people began appearing in all kinds of settings.

I asked a Sister friend of mine, who is versed in dream analysis, to help me make sense of the images. She followed the method of Carl Jung in interpreting dreams. Jung believed that each image in a dream represents something in the one dreaming. When I told my friend about the frequency of African-American men, women, and children in my dreams, she asked me my feelings about black people.

I told her I enjoy being with them, they are relaxing to be with, and I feel at home with them. It then became clear that African-American people in my dreams were a symbol of taking time off; my subconscious was telling me when I needed a break in my ministry. For a year, whenever I had a dream with this image, I immediately scheduled a day off. In fact, this is how I learned how to balance time for ministry and time for play. I believe God gave me this solution to protecting my boundaries; it has never failed me in twenty years of "freelance" work!

In 1985 I asked my provincial for a sabbatical year. I wanted to pursue two main interests: spirituality and issues of social justice. My prayer was going through some radical changes at the time and I felt I needed time to reflect on this. In 1984, I was in South Africa for five weeks giving workshops on the social mission of the church.[3] I wanted to return in order to get a deeper understanding of apartheid and its effects upon all the people, white and black. In addition, I had been traveling to Ireland and giving retreats there for two years. Thus it was that I proposed to spend three months in Ireland, three in Africa—Kenya, Zambia, and South Africa—and end with three more in Ireland. I did not enroll in any kind of a structured program. Contrary to my in-bred need for organization, I decided to do the opposite and just let the year evolve. This would definitely be a challenge!

Having completed all the planning for the sabbatical with plenty of time before departure, I settled back into the retreat work. As time approached, though, to actually leave the country, I began feeling uneasy and not a little anxious about the proposed trip. This is usually the case for me; I feel called to do something and respond with enthusiasm, but then get cold feet as the project gets closer. I was fearful on two counts: the changes in my spiritual life and the way I prayed, and, returning to South Africa. While on vacation, I experienced four revelations of God's protective love, in four different locations. So much was I affected and encouraged by these encounters that I took a photograph of each place, all of which I still have and refer to whenever I am in need of inner strength. Of late, this has been the case in my move from city life to the prairies of southern Alberta and from community life to living alone.

The first revelation took place at Emerald Bay on Lake Tahoe in northern California. In the middle of this beautiful inlet is a small island with the remains of a castle on it. On three sides of the bay are steep mountains and majestic trees. I have been to Emerald Bay many times, even when I was a child, and have always marveled at the loveliness of the area. This time it came to me, "I am the small island and God is the mountains." I am protected.

About a two hour drive from Lake Tahoe there is an expansive, peaceful meadow. Meadows have a special significance for me because they are what I imagine heaven will be like. I had never been to this particular meadow before. It, too, was encompassed by tall trees and mountains. This time it occurred to me that I was the meadow, God the mountains— again, a sense of God protecting me.

Traveling still further, I came to a rise with a viewpoint of a magnificent valley. There were mountains, but no trees. From where I stood, I could see that the mountains sloped gently to the valley floor. The view was breathtaking. Like the two other scenes, a similar message came to me, "You are the valley, I am the mountains, be not afraid."

The fourth revelation happened a couple of weeks later about an hour drive from my home of that time, San Diego. It was my day off and I drove up into the Mount Laguna National Forest. There is a viewpoint I like to visit when I am in that area. From it, you look down two thousand feet to the Anza Borego Desert. There is a barren valley at the bottom, surrounded by towering mountains. By now, I was getting used to the message associated with such landscapes. Perhaps I was given the fourth experience so I wouldn't think the first three were just coincidences. Whatever, the energy from these four episodes is still very much with me fifteen years later.

Only recently, a very perceptive friend of mine, upon hearing of these locations and their effect on me, wondered why God had chosen four very different scenes: a little island, a meadow, a mountain valley, and a desert floor. She suggested they might represent four different emotional-spiritual states. Her insight has expanded my understanding of God's message, that he is there to protect me (us) at all times, in both the good and the difficult, in both the routine and the challenging.

Stories of God's Protection

This desire for protection is a universal human need. As we approached the new millennium, many people were filled with all kinds of fears and anxieties. Some feared worldwide chaos because of Y2K, others saw in floods, hurricanes, and earthquakes a portent of doom, while still others considered the lack of peace in some countries as sure signs of the coming of the end of the world. Those who found comfort and security in dependence on a loving and protective God fared far better, spirit-wise, than those who put their trust in earthly things.

When I am tempted to fall prey to fear I find it helpful to remember the words of the Indian poet, Tagore:

> I thought that my voyage had come to its end at the last limit of my power, that the path before me was closed, that provisions were exhausted and the time come to take shelter in a silent obscurity.

> But I find that thy will knows no end in me. And when old words die out on the tongue, new melodies break forth from the heart; and where the old tracks are lost, new country is revealed with its wonders.[4]

When I asked my lay friends about their experience of the protective love of God, they responded with a variety of interesting stories.

Larry, and Penny can see God's protective presence when they reflect on their life.

Larry relates how God has protected and blessed him:

> I am convinced God has a plan for me. I say this because of several experiences during my four years in the Navy. On two occasions, several of us should have been killed or badly maimed while loading ammunition in preparation for deployment during the Korean War. A second experience occurred while we were firing shells during a heavy bombardment. God's protection permitted ten of us sailors to survive without an explosion that should have happened on the ship due to a faulty firing mechanism.

Penny states:

> The main thing I have discovered about God is that he has a lot more time than I do. God's time is not mine. Often I feel I need an answer to something I've prayed for right away, when it may be years in coming. I know that with the perspective of years, I can see God's constancy and wisdom played out in every life that is close to me. I think it is that realization, more than any other, that builds my faith. I believe that God is watching out for me and mine, and that his direction is what gives meaning to our lives.

Margaret went through a very difficult time after her marriage broke up. She explains:

> I have never been angry with God even though I have experienced many trials. There have been times when I wondered about the crooked lines God was drawing in

my life, but I have always had a certainty of
God's love and protection no matter what
the circumstances. When I was divorced,
raising my two young children alone, and
going through bankruptcy, all at the same
time, I still had a strong faith in God's presence. One year I was unable to afford medical insurance for myself and my children.
Miraculously, we all remained illness-free
that whole year! Even in difficult and very
low times, I was always certain that God was
with us, protecting us, and would not give us
more problems than we could handle.

Psalm 23, "The Lord Is My Shepherd," is a favorite
prayer for many people. Phrases like: "He gives me
new strength . . . he guides me in the right paths . . .
even if I go through the deepest darkness, I will not be
afraid, Lord, for you are with me," and "your shepherd's rod and staff protect me" can give us strength
even in the worst of times.

Al, who is a bachelor, finds this psalm particularly
important on his spiritual journey: "The one passage
in the Bible which speaks most intimately to my heart
is Psalm 23. The image of God as mercy and loving
kindness, tenderly caring for me in spite of my faults
and failings, protecting me from temptation, is clearly
stated." Echoing these insights, Pam recalls how relating to God as shepherd has helped her through some
serious physical maladies:

I have experienced God's protective and
supportive love most powerfully when I had
operations. The first one was some years ago.
I was anxious about the procedure, but God
was so close both before and after the opera-
tion, that I could almost see and touch him in
the hospital room. This feeling gave me a

great deal of peace. When I broke my hip, I was pretty doped up before the doctors operated. However, afterwards, I experienced God's love through friends who showed they cared for me in so many ways, from bringing me cards and flowers in the hospital to suppers and other types of assistance after I returned home; one faithful friend brought me the eucharist almost every day.

Kathy also finds support in the Old Testament, especially in the words from Isaiah 49:13-16:

For the Lord comforts his people
and shows mercy to the affected. . . .
Can a mother forget her infant,
be without tenderness for the child of her womb?
Even should she forget,
I will never forget you,
See, upon the palms of my hands
I have written your name (NAB).

She explains, "When I sing the words of Carey Landry's song based on the passage, I know that I am never alone, that God is always with me no matter what I am going through."[5]

Looking back to their childhood, Terry and Marilyn recall moments of deliverance and protection. Terry writes:

God has always been present in my life, sometimes providing comfort when there was no one else. There were times in my youth when it appeared that no one was in control. My parents divorced when I was five years old and I lived for short periods of time with various relatives. I learned at an early age that I was not part of a family as most other kids were and I felt a great deal of independence and responsibility for myself. However, as a child I almost drowned, was nearly struck by a falling tree, and once came close to running off a twenty-foot cliff. We lived near a forest in British Columbia. I would often go exploring in areas occupied by bears. I would wander along forest pathways in the dark late at night. I even played along some railroad tracks. Yet no harm ever came to me. Somehow, God was taking care of me.

Marilyn relates an incident from her childhood:

I grew up on a farm. When I was eight years old, an employee of my father's tried to abuse me sexually. I was confused, not sure of what was happening but I had a sense of something wrong. A relative of ours walked into the house and the workman quickly stopped what he was doing. I believe God delivered me from serious harm and injury. The man never tried it again. He was fired shortly thereafter, for another reason.

In the Valley of Darkness

Not everyone, of course, experiences deliverance from dangerous situations, be they children or adults. One of the great mysteries of life is why there is so much suffering: why innocent children suffer, why good people are treated violently by others, why innocent people are maimed or killed in war, or why some people die in the middle of what was supposed to be a routine medical procedure. But the reality of suffering doesn't mean we should cease asking God for protection. When we pray in the Lord's Prayer

"Deliver us from evil" we are praying for freedom from the fear of harm (see Chapter Four on the freedom-prayer); ask that a journey be safe; or pray for our children. Even if tragedy strikes, we know that God has a way of entering the experience if we let him.

When Cassie Bernall went to school on April 20, 1999, she had no idea that this would be the last day of her life on earth. Three years before that fateful day at Columbine High School, she was a troubled child. She was, her parents say, a bitter, angry girl obsessed with the occult who regularly dreamed and talked of running away from home, killing her parents, and suicide.[6]

Through the advice of their church's youth group director, her mother and father decided on a steady diet of tough love. Gradually, because of their persistence and the example of the members of the church youth club which Cassie was encouraged to attend, she began to change for the good. However, it wasn't until a weekend youth retreat that her conversion was complete. There, she discovered Christ and his love for her.

One of her friends recalls the change that came over Cassie:

> We were up at Estes Park in the Rockies, about three hundred kids, I'd say. There was a nighttime praise-and-worship service. . . . It was the singing that for some reason just broke down Cassie's walls. It really seemed to change her. . . . We were outside the building, and Cassie was crying. She was pouring out her heart—I think she was praying—and asking God for forgiveness.[7]

Her mother describes how their home life changed as a result of the weekend experience: "From then on, Cassie became a totally different person. She never talked about her weekend, and we never pressed her. But her eyes were bright, she smiled again like she hadn't for years, and she began to treat us . . . with genuine respect and affection." Jesus had descended into her darkness and brought her to the light.

The day of her death was like any day. She was in the library, studying. Suddenly, two of her fellow students burst through the doors and began firing automatic weapons. One student, who was also in the library but who was not harmed during the rampage, saw Cassie hide under a table, her hands clasped in prayer. One of the shooters went up to her and asked if she believed in God. Another student remembers the scene: "Cassie paused, like she didn't know what she was going to answer, and then she said yes. She must have been scared, but her voice didn't sound shaky. It was strong. Then they asked her why, though they didn't give her a chance to answer. They just blew her away."

While her parents continue to mourn the abrupt death of their daughter, they have also reflected extensively on the events of that day. Says her mother, "I know that her death was not a waste, but a triumph of honesty and courage. To me, Cassie's life says that it is better to die for what you believe, than to live a lie. . . ." Cassie could not have predicted it, but her death, as a modern-day martyr, has become an inspiration for young people throughout the United States and Canada. And, for adults too. She certainly inspires me.

Many others over the centuries have faced imprisonment, even death, for their beliefs. When *Time* magazine ran its search for "The Person of the Century" and listed in each issue the names of significant people from various parts of the world, the name that shone brightly for me was Nelson Mandela. Here is a man who so firmly believed in the rightness of his cause that he was willing to spend twenty-five prime years of his life on Robben Island. God did not protect him from going to prison. Instead of emerging a bitter person toward God and those who had persecuted him, he became God's main instrument for beginning healing the hatreds in his country.

In the sixteenth century Christian missionaries went to live among the people of Vietnam. During the years 1820-1840, many Christians were martyred, suffering torments of various kinds for their faith. A letter written in 1843 by Paul Le-Bao-Tinh, an imprisoned martyr, describes his faith in God's love and mercy despite the circumstances of his life:

> I, Paul, in chains for the name of Christ, wish to relate to you the trials besetting me daily, in order that you may be inflamed with love for God and join with me daily in his praises, "for his mercy is forever." The prison here is a true image of everlasting hell: to cruel tortures of every kind—shackles, iron chains, manacles—are added hatred, vengeance, calumnies, obscene speech, quarrels, evil acts, swearing, curses, as well as anguish and grief. But the God who once freed the three children from the fiery furnace is with me always. . . .[8]

Light in the Darkness

No matter how deep our faith, no matter the many great acts of love and compassion we perform, we all hit a "wall" of darkness at some point in our life; a dark valley, a scary forest. Author Victor M. Parachin reflects on six things we can learn in the dark times.

1. In the darkness we yield control of our lives; it is the darkness when we let go of our securities and turn to God.

2. In the darkness we learn to value the light. Often the blessings received and enjoyed are taken for granted until there is deprivation.

3. In the darkness our sense of compassion is heightened. Those who emerge from a dark and difficult time often have a deeper desire to help others who are suffering. There is a strong sense that the suffering should not be wasted.

4. In the darkness we learn more readily. A time of darkness is often when our greatest growth and learning takes place. It is in the dark valley where we simplify life, clarify values, sort out priorities, and discover which friends are true and which are not.

5. In the darkness we are more open to God. The opportunity of seeing clearly is absent in the darkness. Because our vision is blurred, our mind confused and our spirit hurting, we turn to God with a great hunger.

6. In the darkness we learn to live by faith, not merely by sight. During dark and difficult times we acknowledge our helplessness and turn our lives over to God's care and guidance.[9]

The mystic Jessica Powers wrote a poem which describes poignantly both the darkness we encounter and the One we need to rely on in the obscure times of our lives. It is called "The Garments of God."

God sits on a chair of darkness in my soul.
He is God alone, supreme in his majesty.

I sit at His feet, a child in the dark beside Him;
my joy is aware of his glance and my sorrow is
    tempted
to nest on the thought that His face is turned
    from me.
He is clothed in the robes of His mercy,
    voluminous garments—
not velvet or silk and affable to the touch,
but fabric strong for a frantic hand to clutch,
and I hold to it fast with the fingers of my will.
Here is my cry of faith, my deep avowal
to the Divinity that I am dust.
Here is the loud profession of my trust.
I need not go abroad
to the hills of speech or the hinterlands of music
for a crier to walk in my soul where all is still.
I have this potent prayer through good or ill:
here in the dark I clutch the garments of God.[10]

And so we go, through what I call the "4 Ds"—
dryness, darkness, desolation, discouragement—
clinging any way we can to the protective love of God.
God is listening. When I moved to San Diego and a
Jesuit community of four after living for fifteen won-
derfully supportive years in Berkeley, California with
over a hundred Jesuits, my prayer for the first six
months can be summarized in one word, "Help!!"
With God by my side, I eventually adjusted and grew
to love the area and the people.

I moved to San Diego in order to minister, part-
time, at a small church in Tijuana, Mexico. Driving in
a large border city can be hazardous. Every time I left
the United States and drove toward the border, I
asked Our Lady of Guadalupe to protect me from the
other drivers! She did. Though I had some close calls,
in fifteen years I had no accidents.

A sense of being "lost" interiorly came and went, in a regular rhythm, for the first six months after my next major move to an aboriginal reserve in southern Alberta. I had left so much of what was familiar behind—country, culture, climate, Jesuit community life for solitary living, city for prairie. At times I would look out the window of the rectory at the wide expanse of land before my eyes and wonder, "How the heck did I get here?!" But then God would bless me with a dinner invitation from someone on the reserve or someone would drop by just to say hello and chat for awhile and little by little the inner peace triumphed over my inner disquiet. I know for certain I could not have moved here or survived without God's help.

Whenever I start to wonder why we have to go through the darkness as well as the light, I go to an outstanding, short article by fellow Jesuit and friend Phil Blake. The article is called "Learning to Value the Journey." He writes:

> The idea of "journey" is a common spiritual concept. Spiritual writers often speak of the "inner journey," the "path," or the "way." It is an apt metaphor because we are indeed going spiritually from one place to another in this life. . . . At the moment of human conception, a continuum of life begins that will never end. At that point, we commence our walk up the path to the Father. . . . The road we travel is sometimes dark and steep, sometimes broad and sunlit. There are pot holes, and we manage to step into most of them. We have to climb over fallen trees and rock slides to keep going. All these are images of the vicissitudes of our walk with Christ to the Father. . . . It is true that we have "read the last chapter of the book" and that Jesus

Christ has risen from the grave and con-
quered. *There are resurrections in the process of
the spiritual journey, but they are preceded by
agony and death to self* (emphasis added). The
dynamic of "becoming" is a series of dyings
and risings that must be experienced.[11]

Fr. Blake also comments, compellingly, about the
wounds we incur on the journey.

Our radical "yes" [to the journey] has a
transforming effect; it ensures that this
imperfect and flawed effort we make for the
Lord each day is beyond price. Our halting
steps along the way and the wounds we bear
from the journey are beautiful in God's sight.
. . . I am reminded of the example of the tri-
umphant return of the medieval knight from
the wars. The scars on his face and body are
evidence of his valor, and his wounds are his
glory. . . . At the end of our pilgrimage, when
we make that final transition called death,
what we thought might bring us shame will
bring us glory. The scars from the journey
will reflect the splendor and goodness of
God.[12]

Not all of our experiences of needing God's protective love come in the case of dire need. Sometimes,
there is even a bit of humor in this quality of the love
of God, as the following incident shows. At the time,
I was preparing to drive from San Diego to Calgary, a
four day journey. It was the first time I had traveled
by myself in a car for more than two days. My friends
wondered aloud how I, an extrovert, would handle
that much time alone. To make matters worse, the car
did not have cruise control!

Two months before I was to set out on this trip, I
developed a problem with my left foot; plantar

fascitis was the doctor's diagnosis, a painful condition on the bottom of the foot. A month later, the other foot started to hurt as well. Could this be my body's way of telling me it didn't want to make the journey? I asked God for help. One day, in the midst of dealing with these ailments, I was preparing to give a homily on a retreat. The first reading for the Mass was from Deuteronomy 31. The passage concerns Moses who is now over one hundred years old and knows he will not be accompanying the people across the Jordan River to the Promised Land. He wants to assure the people, though, that Yahweh is with them. He tells them: "Be brave and steadfast; have no fear or dread of them [the Amorites, who were enemies of the Israelites], for it is the Lord, your God, who marches with you; he will never fail you or forsake you" (31:6, NAB).

When I first prayed over this passage, my focus was on the Amorites as the "them." However, when I looked for a practical example to illustrate the reading for the retreatants I started to reflect on who was enemy to me. The answer came in a flash: my feet! Here was God answering my prayer, telling me not to worry about the long drive, that he would be with me, "driving" instead of "marching." I felt a great sense of relief. And, curiously, as the date of departure got closer, the left foot healed; in the final week of preparation, the right foot stopped bothering me too. This was a completely new, and unexpected, experience of God's protective love in my life.

Conclusion

We began this chapter with the prophet Isaiah, "When you pass through deep waters, I will be with you; your troubles will not overwhelm you. When you pass through fire, you will not be burned; the hard trials that come will not hurt you" (43:2). Now that we have seen the truth of these words by many personal examples and by your own reflections on your life experience, we conclude with Jesus. In his appeal to the Father for the well-being of his disciples, he prayed:

> I am in the world no more, but these are in the world as I come to you. O Father, most holy, protect them with your name which you have given me. . . . I do not ask you to take them out of the world, but to guard them from the evil one (John 17:11, 15 NAB).

Eight

The Bountiful Love of *God*

All the way to heaven is heaven.

St. Catherine

In Dublin, Ireland, on the grounds of a Jesuit high school, there is a magnificent copper beech tree. It takes three people, with arms outstretched, to encircle its trunk. The tree's hundreds of branches reach out, full of bronze and green colored leaves. Standing at a distance from this grand creation one notices a beautiful symmetry in its stature. However, I think it is the overall *fullness* of the tree that is most impressive. It reminds me of the abundant love of God. Like God's love itself, the tree is overflowing with life.

A few years ago, I made my annual eight day retreat nearby. It was a time in my life when I was experiencing many blessings. As I contemplated the copper beech, I felt inspired to write the following reflection:

> Fullness upon fullness
> upon fullness
> is my life.
> I do not have words adequate
> to describe what is happening in me,

to me, and through me to others.
There are the many friends, the varied places,
the particular graces, all pointing to Someone
greater than each and the sum of all.
Behind it all is a Love
that is beyond my comprehension,
for whom nothing is impossible.
The word I do choose to describe my life,
in the frailty of human language,
is *Bountiful*
and the Source of my bounty
is the lavish Love of God.

*Do you have a favorite image as well that
symbolizes for you the all-encompassing love
of God? Call it (or them) to mind and reflect
on why it speaks so eloquently to your heart.*

Images galore fill the pages of the Bible to illustrate
the fullness of the love of God. From the Old
Testament there are: manna, harvest, fountain of life,
a wedding banquet, cedars of Lebanon, green pas-
tures, springs in dry valleys, a feast of rich food. The
list goes on. The prophet Jeremiah reminds his listen-
ers that God's plan for us is prosperity, not disaster
(29:11). The Song of Songs is a rhapsody of the total,
mutual, love of the Lord and his people; the Lord is
the lover and his people are the beloved. Using the
image of a shepherd to describe the Lord, the psalmist
reminds us "we have everything we need" (Psalm
23:1). Hymns of gratitude for God's abundant goodness, such as in Psalms 103 and 104, raise our minds
and hearts to praise the Lord for his bountiful providence: "He fills my life with good things, so that I stay
young and strong like an eagle" (103:5); "All of them
depend on you to give them food when they need it.
You give it to them, and they eat it; you provide food

and they are satisfied" (104:27-28). We are even given a vision of the fullness of life beyond time: "On this mountain [Zion, symbol of the heavenly Jerusalem] the Lord of hosts will provide for all peoples a feast of rich food and choice wines, juicy, rich food and pure, choice wines" (Isaiah 25:6 NAB).

Moving into the New Testament, St. Paul writes of the breadth and length, height and depth of God's love (Ephesians 3:17-18); how this complete love of God is, daily, pouring itself into our hearts by means of the Holy Spirit (Romans 5:5), so much so that we are being transformed into the likeness of the Lord "in an ever greater degree of glory" (2 Corinthians 3:18); and Paul prays that this bountiful love "will keep on growing more and more" (Philippians 1:9). Peter Hannan points out that, in transforming us "in an ever greater degree of glory," the Bible uses a whole series of images to describe the actions of God shaping, molding, weaving, watching over with tender care, and planning our future.[1]

In the last discourse of John's gospel, Jesus tells his disciples, "I love you just as the Father loves me" (John 15:9). It is difficult for us to grasp the magnitude of what Jesus is saying here, "I love each of you with the same fullness of love that I receive from my Father." We are back to our potential to take in the love of God, which Jesus asks the Father will continue to grow (John 17:26).

When Jesus multiplied the loaves and the fish near the shore of the Lake of Galilee, he gave us a startling symbol of the bounteous love of God. Not only did those present have enough to eat to tide them over until they reached their homes, they had far more than they needed. In the story of the return of the son who had squandered his inheritance while living an immoral life, the picture of his father rushing out to meet the wayward boy and then throwing a party for

him speaks volumes of the "prodigal" love of God.
Webster's Dictionary defines "prodigal" as *extremely
abundant.* Not only is the son welcomed home with a
sense of relief by his parents, but they kill the fatted
calf (evidently the choicest meat on their farm). The
sound of music and dancing is so loud that it can be
heard out on the farm. This poem entitled
"Doxology," by an unknown author, beautifully sums
up this brief journey through the Old and New
Testaments:

> God fills my being to the brim
> with floods of his immensity.
> I drown within a drop of him
> whose sea-bed is infinity.
>
> The Father's will is everywhere
> for chart and chance his precept keep.
> There are no beaches to his care
> nor cliffs to pluck from his deep.
>
> The Son is never far away from me
> for presence is what love compels.
> Divinely and incarnately
> He draws me where his mercy dwells.
>
> And lo, myself am the abode
> of Love, the third of the Triune,
> the primal surge and sweep of God
> and my eternal claimant soon!
>
> Praise to the Father and the Son
> and to the Spirit! May I be,
> O Water, Wave and Tide in One,
> Thine animate doxology.

The thirteenth-century mystic Raymond Lull
(1232-1316) summarizes the whole of our Christian
life in this dialogue in which the beloved of God
explains his very being:

They asked the Lover, "Where do you come from?"

He answered, "From love."

"To whom do you belong?" "I belong to love."

"Who gave birth to you?" "Love."

"Where were you born?" "In love."

"Who brought you up?" "Love."

"How do you live?" "By love."

"What is your name?" "Love."

"Where do you come from?" "From love."

"Where are you going?" "To love."

"Where do you live?" "In love."[2]

Nature's Voice

Through the wisdom of the Blackfoot people (Siksika Nation), I am learning new ways of imaging God and God's creation. *Apistotoki* is the name for the Creator in their language, the Source of creative love. Two realities in particular speak to me, symbolically, of the fullness of love: the four directions and the buffalo. The number four has great significance if one reflects on the many examples of it in creation.[3] Here, the four directions are explained by Long Standing Bear Chief of the Blackfeet Nation in Montana.

> The ceremonial pipe is offered to the four directions, east, south, west, and north, in that order. The pipe is offered above to the Creator and down to Mother Earth. There are spirits in each of the directions who are guardians and watch over the things that are attributed to that direction.
>
> In the direction to the east, for example, some tribes believe the rising sun symbolizes the Creator who begins the day. The sun is

not considered to be the Creator, but is symbolic of the power of the Creator.

The south is looked upon as the direction of youth and where things are made to grow. As the sun goes across the sky then the plants turn in that direction.

The west is the direction from which the storms and water comes. The water is sacred and a precious gift the Creator has given to all life. We cannot live without water.

The north is the direction of our old age. It is white. It symbolizes the wisdom that is borne by the elderly, the generations gone before us. It is also looked upon as the direction the winter weather comes to put things to rest for awhile to be born again in the spring.[4]

The buffalo (*Enee*, in Blackfoot, meaning bison), which roamed the plains in the millions a hundred years ago, expresses the bountiful love of God because it provided aboriginal people with everything they needed for food, clothing, shelter, tools, and ceremony. Long Standing Bear Chief explains:

The shoulder blade of the animal became a hoe. The ribs when tied together in a special way, made a sled for small children to play with during the winter. The tanned hide covered the people with warmth. The hide, when used ceremonially, was cut up and painted different colors and used as an offering in the Sun Dance. . . . The bones were crushed and the marrow boiled out and added to dried meat and berries to make pemmican, a very nutritious food. . . . Many bones were shaped into arrowheads, awls, and other kinds of tools.[5]

Nature acclaims the fullness of the love of God in the immensity of her oceans and seas, in the majesty of her mountains, in her glorious sunrises and sunsets, in the northern lights, in the grandeur of a copper beech tree or a giant redwood. We celebrate the great love that created all this in the Psalms, in song, in all the arts, and in poetry. One of my favorite songs is "How Great Thou Art."[6]

Do you have a special song or poem that raises your heart and spirit?

One of the joys of moving to southern Alberta is the opportunity to meet people whose line of work existed formerly for me only in books I had read. Such a person is Lloyd Dolen who is both a cowboy and a poet.

I have had the pleasure of visiting with him and his wife Norma at their ranch an hour outside of Calgary. Their warm hospitality is one of the ways I have experienced God's bountiful love. Here, Lloyd shares his experience of the divine in nature in a poem called "A Cowboy and His Soul."

There is nothing to compare with the tang of
autumn air
in the foothills of the Rockies, at the early wake
of dawn.
Just the stillness of the night breeze, and the
rustle of the leaves.
A lone calf breaks the silence, bawling for its
mom.
As I stood in awesome wonder, at the beauty
there before me
and I started down the trail, across nature's
domain

I watched a mama coyote, leading her young
	family
to a place she could hunt and wander, and a
	home that she could claim.

Nature warned about the winter, that would
	come and go
in the stillness of the forest, and the hush of
	falling snow.
Like a mantel it falls, in the stillness of the night
covering the hills and valley, in a blanket of
	shimmering white.

Have you ever seen the magic display, of hoar
	frost on the trees?
Have you felt the sting of winter, in a northern
	arctic breeze?
Have you watched the northern lights, and how
	they dance on high
or watched a winter sunset, light up a purple
	sky?

The winter beauty disappears, with a warm
	spring breeze.
Water runs down the mountain slope, and leaves
	adorn the trees.
The birds are singing love songs, that no juke box
	can compare,
and the fragrant smell of wild flowers, flow
	gently in the air.

The fabric of creation can be found in nature's
	loom,
beneath the watchful eye, of a silver smiling
	moon.
I watch nature's beauty as it slumbers through
	the night,
and contemplate God's creation, and the night
	owl on its flight.

Summer days are here and you hope the time is
near
to live again close to the earth, and bless the land
that gave you birth.
You can ride through the forest cool, or sit beside
some limpid pool
and watch a trout jump for a fly, or see a lone
cloud floating by.

Or watch a humming bird on wing,
then you will know that you have been out
where the West begins,
and you've had time to ponder on how nature
plays it's role,
in the land God gives to a cowboy and his soul.

More Voices of Praise

When I asked my friends about their experience of
this manifestation of God's love, they shared a variety
of examples from their lives. Pam, who has made the
eight-day Ignatian retreat, says:

My experience with the Spiritual Exercises of
St. Ignatius began the process of seeking to
"find God in all things." I find that as I see
God in people, places, and events more keep
getting added to the list! I see God's creative
love in all of nature, from every mountain
and tree down to the smallest creature or
blade of grass. Even inanimate things speak
to me of God's love.

Penny relates how she hears God in the words and
voices of children, in the music of nature, and in the
perfect silence of a moment. Susan describes how she
experiences the voice of God in music—sacred, opera,
popular, instrumental, classical. So much variety in

sound, she admits she can be moved to tears of gratitude to God by a particular piece.

The eucharist is where Bev finds the fullness of God's love: "For me to be who God wants me to be and do what he wants me to do, no matter what obstacles arise, is the best goal I can achieve in my life; to attain this goal, I need his ongoing help and I find this help most of all in the eucharist." My friend Denny suggested the following as a title for this book: "A God of Many Loaves."

> God feeds us in so many ways, both physically and spiritually, every single day. Everything we receive comes from God. All the corporal works of mercy are God's gifts to us. Also, the passage in scripture where the Father even knows the numbers of hairs of our head (Luke 12:7). In this age of computerized information, the size of God's database is way beyond our imagination!

Ken and Mary Ann share their wonderment in terms of their respective marriages. Ken has been married to his high school sweetheart, Margaret, for fifty-eight years. "When I was a young man, I could not have dreamed that at the age of seventy-eight I would feel so excited about my life. Margaret and I have a wonderful friendship. I experience God loving me in abundance through her love."

Mary Ann has been married for two years. She relates her experience:

> I have truly felt the greatest amount of God's love for me through his gift of my husband. I know that in this man, our Lord has provided me with a companion to share in God's gifts, a man who exemplifies and personifies God's love for me. Through the sacrament of marriage, I see God as One who encourages happiness both on earth and in

heaven. I always thought of myself as a
happy person, but until God united me with
my husband, I was afraid to let myself go to
the *full* joy of living. I now experience God's
love as approving and liberating . . . allowing
me to wallow in the love and happiness he
wants us to have and to share.

Terry, who is in his early fifties, reflects on the fullness of the love of God, at this time of his life:

I am now sitting at what my wife likes to
refer to as her mid-life (assuming she will
live to be a hundred!) and I have all the temporal treasures a person could want. I have
been married for twenty-nine years. My wife
and I still love and care for each other deeply.
We have two nearly grown sons, who make
us very proud. We have a family for whom
we care deeply and who care for us. We are
part of a vibrant faith community where we
are free to worship and share in the love of
God. We are blessed with friendships that
span thirty years. And, we have a small family business that provides for all our material needs, that also allows us to share some of
our good fortune with others. We have lived
through some difficult times as a family and
have needed help at different points along
the way; the help has always been there. We
feel truly blessed by God.

Al reiterates this sense of feeling blessed, especially as he reflects on this phrase in the Good Shepherd
Psalm (23), "there is nothing I shall want" (NAB).

Sometimes an awareness of the bountiful love of
God comes immediately after a time of inner darkness. Kathy relates such an experience:

One morning I awakened and felt a great sense of aloneness. I felt God was very distant from me. It bothered me more than usual. I want to feel his presence, but get very discouraged when I don't and wonder if there is something lacking in me. That morning I went to Mass and the priest read the entrance antiphon, which is not normally read at our parish. The passage spoke of not giving up in our attempts to be closer to God! What a coincidence, I thought! This "coincidence" made me feel God as very present and that he is always present in my life, even if I am not aware of it.

Nancy-Jean and Bob, parents of three delightful children, own a sheep ranch in southern Alberta. When I asked them how they experience the fullness of God's love they responded in the following way. Nancy-Jean:

I think that the socially acceptable answer would be—through my children and husband, the great place I live, the volunteer work I do, and so forth. However, deep inside I struggle against giving a simple, sweet, "isn't everything wonderful between God and me" kind of answer, no matter how true. The fact is most days I never give the fullness of God's love any thought. When faced with the direct question, I realize that the times I feel engulfed by God's love are usually after I've crashed from stress, worry, fatigue, rage, or physical or emotional pain. God's love revives my spirit, in the same way it says in Psalm 23, "The Lord is my Shepherd," and gives me hope to get up and keep going.

Interestingly, her husband Bob's response was in a similar vein. He explains:

> When bad things happen I begin to think that's all that's going on in my life, but then I notice something good, like my family or the beautiful pastoral setting where we live, and I realize that there is more good going on than I thought. That's when I experience the fullness of the love of God. And this realization is what gives me hope.

In preparing to write this chapter I came across three additional stories that speak to the abundance of God's love. The first is from Jacque Braman who, in responding to the question "How can I find God?" wrote:

> I first found God as a child. But since I wasn't really looking for him it would be more accurate to say that God found me. I was raised in the United Methodist Church, went to Sunday school every week, learned all the Bible stories, and pretty much accepted them as truth. After all, I had no reason not to believe. Then God, one night as I was riding in the car, gave me some tangible proof. It was a peaceful evening. My mom and brother and sister and I were on our way to a high school basketball game that my dad was coaching. It was quiet in the car. The others may have been talking some, but not to me. I was just looking out the window at the still night, enjoying the stars, and the street lights, and happy to be on my way to the game. Then a strange thing started to happen. The happiness that I was feeling grew deeper and richer and fuller, and completely overwhelmed me, even though I still felt

quiet and peaceful. Then I noticed that tears were rolling down my cheeks. This was really weird. I double-checked: No, I wasn't sad. I had a huge grin plastered on my face, one that was beyond my ability to remove, try as I might. . . .

Then I understood. This was how full joy could be. This was a joy that comes only from God. I relished the moment, immersed in joy, filled with thankfulness and contentment. I shared my thoughts with God in silent prayer, and knew he was right there with me.[7]

Father Bernie Bush is a Jesuit. In his forty-eight years since entering the order, he has led a very full life. He has been a retreat director, sculptor, private pilot, psychological therapist, and spiritual director. He has also helped turn the olive crop at the Jesuit retreat house where he lives and works into olive oil. Does he ever find life at the retreat house, where he has been for six years, boring? "Never," he says. "Exciting things happen here—interior things. Life here is like falling into a tub of God."[8]

The third story comes from Linda Gall, who explains her life and her experience of God in her own words:

My husband and I are immigrants from the Netherlands and we have twelve children. During World War II we lived through five years without freedom and even with hunger before we were married. Then there were days of homesickness, operations, and pain; exhaustion was no stranger to us either. Today our six daughters and six sons are all married and we have twenty-four grandchildren, up to now! I feel like the flower I put in a vase (a Dutch woman has to have at least one all the time). I love it into life, almost, and I am delighted every time I look at it. God made me as that flower. He looks at me and is delighted.[9]

The Abundance of Abundance

We can see that the bountiful love of God encompasses all the other loves we have considered thus far. Sometimes, if we listen closely, we can hear God saying *personally* to us what Jesus heard after he was baptized, "you are my dear one in whom I am well pleased." After we have done something we are especially ashamed of such as falling into an old sin or some addiction, we can take heart from the words of the poet George Herbert as he reflects on the *unconditional* and *merciful* love of God:

Love bade me welcome; yet my soul drew back,
    Guilty of dust and sin.
But quick-eyed Love, observing me grow slack
    From my first entrance in,
Drew nearer to me, sweetly questioning,
    If I lacked anything.

"A guest," I answered, "worthy to be here."
    Love said, "You shall be he."
"I, the unkind, ungrateful? Ah, my dear,
    I cannot look on thee."
Love took my hand, and smiling did reply,
    "Who made thy eyes but I?"

"Truth, Lord, but I have marred them; let my
        shame
    Go where it doth deserve."

"And know you not," says Love, "who bore the
    blame?"
    "My dear, then I will serve."
"You must sit down," says Love, "and taste my
    meat."
    So I did sit and eat.

God's loving *providence* can come to us in the most
unexpected of ways. This happened to one man I met
through a parish mission. I came into contact with
Craig through his mother, Cathie, who was attending
the mission. She told me that Craig, who was in his
early forties at the time, had recently found out he had
cancer and asked if I would have time to speak with
him. We met a week later. During this initial visit he
told me he was not only suffering physically, but also
emotionally and spiritually. He shared how he had a
lot of painful memories related to his father
(deceased) and how he treated Craig as a child. When
I asked him about his faith-life, he admitted he had
not been to church in a long time. He looked miser-
able as he said something that quite startled me,
"something drastic had to happen to wake me up, I
guess cancer is the answer."

I suggested he do two things: see a psychologist I
know who is especially good in helping men deal
with father wounds and do a thorough examination
of his life in order to go to confession. He agreed. A
week later we met again. He told me he had contact-
ed the counselor and made an appointment. With
genuine sorrow and trust in God's mercy, he made a
general confession. It was deeply moving for both of
us and a great burden seemed to lift from his heart.
He left that day smiling for the first time since I had
met him. I was not to see him again for three months,
though we did keep in touch by letter. When we met
again he told me the counselor had been a great help

and that he had made his peace with his father. He said he had been attending Sunday Mass ever since we first got together. Emotionally and spiritually, he had undergone significant changes for the better and it showed both on his face and in the way he talked.

Meanwhile, he had come to a new crossroads with the disease and wanted to discuss it with me. He shared, "I have an important decision to make, whether or not to undergo chemotherapy; I am leaning in the direction of not doing it." We discussed the pros and cons of the treatment, its side effects, etc. He told me he'd let me know his decision. He thanked me for journeying with him through this ordeal and for being God's instrument in bringing him to the inner peace he now experienced. I received a letter from him a few months later, one that I will always treasure. The letter was written two days before he died. He wrote that he had decided not to go through chemotherapy, that the cancer had taken a strong hold on his body, but that he was at peace with himself and with God. However, what he most wanted to share with me was something that happened the day before he wrote. He was lying in bed. It was morning. Suddenly, Jesus appeared at the foot of his bed. His arms were opened wide, welcoming Craig home. He was completely filled with joy as he beheld Jesus.

He asked his mother to send the letter to me. In a separate note, she said he died peacefully. She and I still marvel at the extraordinary inner transformation Craig had gone through in a relatively short time. I consider him to be one of my angels, guiding and protecting me in my new, Canadian home. So, you might say, providence has touched us both.

Sometimes God's *freeing* and *healing* love go hand in hand in a person's life. Such is the case with a religious sister who was a student in a class on Christian spirituality that I teach in a summer degree program.

Each student is required to write a faith autobiography, showing the connection between what they learned in the course with their own faith experience. Sister Bernice had entered the Benedictine order after being a mother and grandmother and encountered a great many difficulties along the way. She decided to include in the paper her own personal magnificat. Inspired by Mary, who praised God for the blessings she received (Luke 1:46-55), Sister honored God in her own way. Here is an excerpt from what she composed.

> Praise to you, Abba, my Father,
> and to Your Son, Jesus Christ, my Savior,
> for you have done great things for me.
> My heart, my soul, my very being
> grumbled and groaned all the days of my life.
>
> I was blind, my eyes could not see.
> I was deaf, my ears could not hear.
> My body was numb, I could not feel.
> I cried out to my heavenly Father. . . .
> Thank you Father, for you have heard the cry of
>   the lowly one.
> You took me, and in the sun we walked.
> Then terror struck me, you left me
> in the depths of darkness, my very life laid before
>   me.
> Fear gripped my heart.
>
> At the waterways of life,
> as a spiritual child you beckoned me on.
> I placed my trust in You, my God.
> Across the bridges and water currents I crossed,
> my very being trembling as I looked down.
> In your compassion you whispered to fear not.
> Upon crossing you gave me your Son, my
>   brother, Jesus,
> who took my hand and walked with me.

He touched my eyes, so that I might see him. . . .
He touched my ears, to hear him speak. . . .
He touched my being, so that I might feel the
    touch of his love. . . .

As the rain now falls upon me, as the wind
    whips my face
and the coldness sets in, I have no fear,
For your love, my Lord, surrounds me.

The protective love of God is seen in its abundance in the following two stories. Roy and Judy have a cattle ranch in southern Alberta. Beauty abounds in the many colorful wildflowers that grow on their land: the purple shooting stars, spring crocus, sticky geraniums, calypso orchids, blue bells, larkspur, and Alberta's signature, the wild rose. Hiking on their ranch is a sensual delight of color and fragrance. Nearby, Jumping Pound Creek, with its bull trout and rocky mountain whitefish, flows lazily along. Their home rests on a bluff, with a spectacular view of the Rocky Mountains.

In the midst of this tranquil setting came a terrifying experience. Their four children, ranging in age at the time from eleven to eighteen, prepared for an evening of study while their parents went out for dinner. The children settled themselves in the family room, in the basement quarters. Roy told me recently how, when the house was built, he had insisted to the builders that there be an outside door to the basement; they had been reluctant but, he insisted. "Something spurred me on," he said. Judy and Roy saw the smoke first and then the flames. Their initial fear that this could be coming from their home was replaced with terror when they realized it was their house on fire and where were the children?! There was no sign of the fire department. The parents couldn't get in through the front door because of the intensity of the blaze. Roy went in through a side door and managed to get upstairs to the bedrooms. No one was there. He raced back outside and, thank God, found his children—shaken but safe, recuperating on the lawn.

They related to their parents what had happened. What alerted them to possible danger was the sound of the smoke alarms in the kitchen. The youngest set out to investigate. As she started up the stairs toward the kitchen she saw that it was engulfed in flames. She ran back downstairs and alerted her siblings. Each escaped, unharmed, through the basement door their father had insisted on having. Had the door not been there, they would not have survived. Despite the total loss of the house and all their possessions in it, Roy looks philosophically at the event: "We lost our house which can be replaced. Our children are safe and they are far more important to us than things." Reflecting now on the fire, Judy says, "You have to get on with life after such an experience, but you don't get over it."

Arizona Senator John McCain relates an experience that provides a second example of the abundance of God's protective love. Shot down during the Vietnam War, he spent five and a half years in a prison camp. Speaking of his ordeal in much the same way as St. Peter might have explained his jail tribulation (Acts 12), Senator McCain shares one experience from his time of imprisonment. He speaks here in the third person.

> Many years ago a scared American prisoner of war in Vietnam was tied in torture ropes by his tormentors and left alone in an empty room to suffer through the night. Later in the evening, a guard he had never spoken to entered the room and silently loosened the ropes to relieve his suffering. Some months

later, on Christmas morning, as the prisoner
stood alone in the prison courtyard, the same
Good Samaritan walked up to him and stood
next to him for a few moments. Then with
his sandal, the guard drew a cross in the
dirt.[10]

Conclusion

We have considered many images and experiences
of the fullness of God's love in this chapter, this God
"in whom we live and move and have our being"
(Acts 17:28). As my friend Bill Spohn, says: "It isn't
the mountaintop we go to find God, but into the stuff
of everyday life. By appreciating ordinary time in its
depths, the places where it touches the boundaries,
we meet the mystery and depth of the encompassing
presence of God." Or, as a Latin American poet put it
so well:

I searched for God in the heavens,
but I found he had fallen to earth.
So now I must search for him among my
    friends.[11]

There is a traditional devotion that has fallen on
hard times lately, to the Sacred Heart of Jesus, God
with a human heart. "Among all the signs which
serve to express human love," writes Fr. Edouard
Glotin, "the symbol of the heart is one of the most intimate and the most delicate." It is also one of the most
abundant. Fr. Glotin continues, "The revelation which
Jesus has made of his Heart is the sign of an overwhelming friendship for the Church and for each one
of the faithful in particular." The Heart of Jesus
expresses what is most ineffable in the gift God makes
to us of the divine nature. It is the pierced Christ that
most captures the imagination of Fr. Glotin. He

writes, "The sign of the pierced side, from which flowed blood and water, expresses in fact the fruitfulness of the act of redemption. . . . It was for love that Christ died, and it is from his wounded heart that, under the symbol of living water, love still flows. . . . The paschal mystery in its totality is a mystery of love."[12] Could we not say, then, that the Heart of Christ speaks profoundly of God's bountiful love? Perhaps it is St. Paul who sums it up best:

> I pray that Christ will make his home in your hearts through faith. I pray that you may have your roots and foundation in love, so that you, together with all God's people, may have the power to understand how broad and long, how high and deep, is Christ's love. Yes, may you come to know his love—although it can never be fully known—and so be completely filled with the very nature of God (Ephesians 3:17-19).

Nine

The Everlasting Love of God

The mountains and hills may crumble,
but my love for you will never end;
I will keep forever my promise of peace.

ISAIAH 54:10

A few years ago I had a three-hour lunch with a Jesuit friend of mine. What makes this memory so clear is that during our visit, my good friend of thirty-two years shared that he would be leaving the Jesuits and that he was planning to get married. He had been on a leave of absence for a year. I had hoped this time of reflection would result in a return to community rather than a separation. That evening at dinner news reached the Jesuits I was staying with at the time that another well known member of our Province had decided to take a leave of absence. Both of these men were excellent teachers and very effective in their respective ministries. They both had obvious leadership qualities; either one was capable of leading the Province. Needless to say, the rest of us were stunned. Personally, I felt like an earthquake had happened inside of me. As I sought to make sense of this devastating news from these two fellow priests, I was led by the Holy Spirit to a grace that has had a profound impact on my spiritual life.

The new knowledge came through an article that I had started reading on what we Jesuits call, "The Examen of Conscience."[1] The first idea that caught my eye came in the author's reflection on present day American Jesuits, that many of us have an existential fear of alienation and abandonment, as real as that of any other American.[2] As I reflected on the impact my two Jesuit friends' decisions had on me, I began to wonder if I might have a fear of abandonment. After all, if two men of such caliber were in the process of choosing another vocation, what was to keep me a Jesuit? This was an existential fear—about my basic humanity—and not something I could relegate to my childhood.

I decided to ask God for help, for an antidote of faith to counter any fear of being abandoned by God. An answer came two weeks later while I was directing a retreat. I woke up one morning and clear as crystal these words came: "Max, my love for you is everlasting. It's not for ten years or twenty or thirty, it's forever." I felt a profound sense of peace at this divine disclosure; all fears of being abandoned vanished in an instant. I found myself responding to God in return, "And my love for you is everlasting." My inner, spiritual, stability returned and I found my commitment to being a Jesuit stronger than ever.

The everlasting love of God is seen clearly in the New Testament. On his last journey to Jerusalem, Jesus frequently spoke to his disciples of his approaching passion and death, but always with an additional note of encouragement and hope. In words like, "but three days later he will rise to life" and "on the third day the Son of Man will rise again," he prepared them for the days following his crucifixion. When Peter expressed the total commitment of the

disciples to following Jesus by leaving their very
homes, Jesus responded, "I assure you that anyone
who leaves home or wife or brothers or sisters or parents or children for the sake of the Kingdom of God
will receive much more in this present age and eternal
life in the age to come" (Luke 18:29-30).

St. Paul has many references to everlasting life in
his letters. The passages that have influenced my own
faith are those in which he speaks of Jesus' resurrection and then of our own. "I passed on to you what I
received . . ." he wrote in 1 Corinthians 15:3-4, "that
Christ died for our sins, as written in the scriptures;
that he was buried and that he was raised to life three
days later. . . ." Further along in the same chapter, he
wrote, " . . . the truth is that Christ has been raised
from death, as the guarantee that those who sleep in
death will also be raised" (15:20). After encouraging
the Philippians to persevere in their faith, he wrote:
"We, however, are citizens of heaven, and we eagerly
wait for our Savior, the Lord Jesus Christ, to come
from heaven. He will change our weak mortal bodies
and make them like his own glorious body, using that
power by which he is able to bring all things under his
rule" (3:20-21). This, of course, is great cause for hope.
As he wrote in his first letter to the Thessalonians:
"Our brothers and sisters, we want you to know the
truth about those who have died, so that you will not
be sad, as are those who have no hope. We believe
that Jesus died and rose again, and so we believe that
God will take back with Jesus those who have died
believing in him. . . . And so we will always be with
the Lord" (4:13-14, 17).

Although it is generally held by biblical scholars
that the idea of individual survival after death is not
present in the Old Testament, there are some passages
that seem to express a striving for some form of after-
life, for example, Isaiah 53:10-12.[3] There, the prophet

writes: "The Lord says, 'It was my will that he should suffer; his death was a sacrifice to bring forgiveness. And so he will see his descendants; he will live a long life, and through him my purpose will succeed. After a life of suffering, he will again have joy; he will know that he did not suffer in vain.'" It is in the book of Daniel that the first clear expression of the hope of resurrection occurs, however.[4] In his vision by the Tigris River, an angel tells Daniel about the end of time:

> When that time comes, all the people of your nation whose names are written in God's book will be saved. Many of those who have already died will live again: some will enjoy eternal life, and some will suffer eternal disgrace (12:1–2).

We have the advantage of considering Old Testament texts from the viewpoint of Jesus' resurrection and ascension. Many times I, and others who have shared their prayer experiences with me, have found spiritual nourishment about God's everlasting love in them. Beginning with the book of Genesis where it speaks of the covenant between Yahweh and Noah, we are told that this is an everlasting bond between Yahweh and all living creatures (9:16). Later, Yahweh tells Abraham, "I will keep my promise to you and to your descendants in future generations as an everlasting covenant" (17:7). In 2 Samuel, God speaks to David through the prophet, Nathan, telling him that his kingdom will last forever (7:16). David's last words are, indeed, about the divine pledge he has received: "God will bless my descendants because he has made an eternal covenant with me, an agreement that will not be broken, a promise that will not be changed" (2 Samuel 23:5). When the people are tempted to think that God has deserted them, the prophet Isaiah is sent to remind the people of his enduring love: "Can a woman forget her own baby and not love the child she bore? Even if a mother should forget her child, I will never forget you" (49:15). Even if the mountains and hills collapse, Yahweh reassures the Israelite people (and us) that his love will never end (54:10).

One of the words that is often used in the psalms to speak about this quality of God's love is *steadfast*. Depending on the biblical translation, *constant* is used interchangeably with steadfast. In Psalm 36:5, the author declares, "Lord, your constant love reaches the heavens; your faithfulness extends to the skies." The psalmist relies on the constant love of God (13:5); he rejoices because of the constant love he has felt in times of trouble and sorrow (31:7-10), and he places his trust on this steadfast love of God to protect him from his enemies and those who persecute him (Psalm 31:14-16) (see also Psalm 62:11 and 89:1-4).

Jeremiah and Hosea also turn our minds and hearts toward the everlasting love of God. As Israel begins the journey home after being exiled in Babylon, the Lord tells the people, "I have always loved you, so I continue to show you my constant love. Once again, I will rebuild you" (Jeremiah 31:3-4). In the second chapter of Hosea, the account of Yahweh and his people is told in terms of a love story, a romance gone bad because of Israel's unfaithfulness. Here, Yahweh is addressing the people with his relentless love:

> I will allure her [Israel], and bring her into the wilderness and speak tenderly to her. There she shall respond as in the days of her youth, as at the time when she came out of the land of Egypt. . . . I will take you for my wife forever; I will take you for my wife in righteousness and in justice, in steadfast love

and in mercy. I will take you for my wife in
faithfulness; and you shall know the Lord
(Hosea 2:14-15, 19 NRSV).

With the New Testament came the new covenant.
It was primarily expressed by Jesus in the Sermon on
the Mount, especially in the Beatitudes, which he
taught by both word and action. The new covenant
does not replace the old, but fulfills it. God's steadfast
love is the same as in the Old Testament. The
eucharistic Jesus' gift of the new covenant is his very
body and blood. As a priest, I have become very
aware of its significance. The eucharist is a sign of the
everlasting covenant between God and humanity and
all creation. Not only that, it is a pledge of the glory to
come.[5] It is the risen Christ who invites us to the
sacred meal and feeds us with his word and his body
and blood. Pope John Paul II expressed this truth well
in his Apostolic Letter, *Dies Domini*: "At the table of
the Bread of Life, the Risen Lord becomes really, sub-
stantially, and enduringly present through the memo-
rial of his Passion and Resurrection and the Bread of
Life is offered as a pledge of future glory" (#39). As
Jesus himself said: "I am the living bread that came
down from heaven. If anyone eats this bread, he/she
will live forever. . . . Whoever eats my flesh and drinks
my blood has eternal life, and I will raise him/her to
life on the last day" (John 6:51, 54). This is truly a
pledge of everlasting love.

When I asked my lay friends about their experience of the everlasting love of God, they responded in
the following ways. Davey captures well the notion of
the relentless care of God:

> I suppose one could go on and on picking
> out events and symbols of God's love, but in
> the end I feel it is the patience of God, his
> faith in us, the forgiveness he shows to us,

and the guiding hand he offers us. We can strike that hand, push it away. We can sneer and curse God when things don't go our way. We can argue the validity of miracles. We can question and rationalize the words of the Bible to suit our twentieth century ideas. We can do everything we can to destroy God's love, but to no avail. The love just keeps coming at us. God never gives up.

Penny shares:

God's love is constant and it is wise. I know that with the perspective of years I can see God's constancy and wisdom played out in every person that is close to me. I think it is this realization, more than any other, that helps my faith to grow, that God is watching out for me and mine and that his direction not only gives meaning to our life but is leading us to eternal life.

Alluding to Psalm 139, which speaks of God knowing us before we were born, Margaret reflects, "God has held me in the palm of his hand from the beginning of my existence and will continue to do so well past my time on this earth." In a similar vein, Larry experiences God's love through his human family:

I have had the good fortune to know in my head and my heart that God loves me. I know this because he has shown his love for me by my being born into the family he chose for me. We had a faith-filled home life. I was one of five children; I felt we were equally loved by both our parents. Faith and love characterized our life together.

Reflecting on God's manner of loving, Bev responds:

> Wouldn't it be nice if we creatures could fully understand just one of God's ways of loving! No matter how hard we try, or how long, we run into an "infinite wall" upon which we read the divine message, "I invite you to proceed a little farther in fathoming my love, but there is so much more!"

The Resurrection: The Path to Eternity

To any Christian, no event in the life of Christ or in the life of the church is more important than the resurrection. The resurrection lies at the heart of the faith, containing within it the promise of eternal life. Death is not the last word! In his book *Our Greatest Gift: A Meditation on Dying and Caring*, Henri Nouwen wrote beautifully of the intimate connection between Jesus' resurrection and the love of God. "Through the resurrection, God is saying to Jesus, 'You are indeed my Beloved Son and my love is everlasting,' and to us, 'You are indeed my beloved children and my love is everlasting'. . . . The resurrection reveals to us that love is stronger than death."[6]

A few years ago, I met a man at a parish mission I was presenting. On the last evening he gave me a gift, a poem he had written during the mission. He told me he had been inspired to write when I suggested in one of the conferences that the first person Jesus would have appeared to after the resurrection was his mother. What he wrote is one of the most touching reflections on Jesus' whole life that I have seen.

EASTER S FIRST EMBRACE

Through the Holy Spirit, came Love's incarnate
  light,
cradled in her loving arms,
the blissful babe slept in silent night.

Drawn to Jerusalem's journey, life's commitment
  made,
at the foot of the cross, our redemption paid.
Only memories of Love's past,
she holds but tattered remains.
The struggle with sin dims the light,
shames the day into the darkness of night.

"Look what they have done to my Son!"
Immaculate heart weeping, pierced by evil's
  sword,
O Virgin full of grace,
teach us the power of love endured.

Rejoice, Rejoice, the Son is risen!
"We have seen the Lord!"
Our Father's greatest promised morning,
has put an end to our mother's mourning.

O dawn of Easter morning bliss,
Jesus greets his mother's kiss.
Love to love in Easter's first embrace,
springs forth forever, salvation's grace.

O joyful reconciled peace,
Spirit of Christ, now guide us to the eternal feast.
Amen.

Even in this life, all the graces we have and will
receive—all the healing, freeing, enlightening, recon-
ciling, humbling, empowering love and on and on—
flow through the resurrection. Take Peter as one
prime example. We know his story well. In the midst
of Jesus' passion not only did he deny his master three

times, but he hid in the Upper Room for fear that the
same fate might befall him. As one spiritual writer
portrays it:

> Peter was never a man of neutral colors. In
> the gospel accounts he proclaims with great
> bravado all that he will do for Jesus. But
> Jesus, knowing what is in every man and
> woman corrects him. "Peter, you don't
> understand why I have to die. Without my
> death, you would remain subject to the
> weakness that prevents you from carrying
> out your good intentions. You must come to
> see that, because of your fallen condition,
> your tendency is to deny me instead of deny-
> ing yourself. Only when you realize your
> weakness will you finally give up your life
> and let me transform you by the power of
> my resurrection."[7]

For many years, one of my favorite New
Testament passages was Philippians 3:10: "I wish to
know Christ and the power flowing from his resurrection." These words were especially significant
when I was facing a personal or ministerial challenge,
feeling at the same time an acute awareness of my
humanity. Always, *always*, after praying this passage,
I would feel empowered to do what I was intending.
In that same chapter, Paul writes that by participating
also in the sufferings of Christ, he hopes to "be raised
from death to life" (3:11). And that is of course our
ultimate desire, to take up our "citizenship" in heav-
en (Philippians 3:20). As St. Paul further relates,
"[Christ] will change our weak mortal bodies and
make them like his own glorious body, using that
power by which he is able to bring all things under his
rule" (Philippians 3:21).

We don't know what heaven is like. We use images like light and peace and an indescribable joy to try to capture something of the mystery that awaits us. Is it a physical location or a state of being? Using the age-old notion of heaven as a kind of paradise, Beatrice Bruteau reflects: "Paradise means the great bliss of being at the Heart, being consciously in God, being at the foundation and core of all Being, Unity, Truth, Goodness, and Beauty, being one's real self, being enlightened, being free. It also means the liberating joy of realizing the divine unconditional love."[8]

Evangeline Patterson ponders the effect heaven will have on our self-image:

And that will be heaven
and that will be heaven
and that will be heaven
at last—the first unclouded seeing
to stand like the sunflower

turned full face to the sun, drenched
in light, in the still centre
held, while the circling planets
hum with an utter joy

seeing and knowing
at last, in every particle
seen and known, and not turning away
never turning away again[9]

Whatever unique delights God has in store for the faithful ones, the poet Jessica Powers envisions a homecoming like we've never even been close to experiencing in our temporal sojourn.

The spirit, newly freed from earth,
is all amazed at the surprise
of her belonging: suddenly
as native to eternity
to see herself, to realize

the heritage that lets her be
at home where all this glory lies.

By naught foretold could she have guessed
such welcome home: the robe, the ring,
music and endless banqueting,
these people hers; this place of rest
known, as of long remembering
herself a child of God and pressed
with warm endearments to his breast.[10]

This hunger for heaven for the Christian is not to
be an escape from earthly cares, but rather a cause for
hope. This was expressed well at the Second Vatican
Council in the document *The Church in the Modern
World*: "the expectation of a new earth must not weak-
en but rather stimulate our concern for cultivating
this one. . . . to the extent that [earthly progress] can
contribute to the better ordering of human society, it is
of vital concern to the kingdom of God" (#39). As
Franciscan Michael Guinan explains: "Since harmony
and abundance characterize the new creation, which
has already begun, we are to live that way right now.
If God's kingdom is one of peace, justice, life and love,
our behavior should manifest this now. . . . The vision
of new heavens and a new earth is not just a source of
joy and consolation, but also a challenge to us in the
way we live."[11] And, this commitment, an essential
dimension of our response of love to God, is not only
to other human beings but to all that God has created.

A Final Reflection

The considerations in this chapter on the everlasting love of God are a fitting conclusion to what has
been for me, a labor of love. So profound has been my
personal experiences of the love of God that to write a
book on this theme is one way to thank God for all he

has given me. It is an inexhaustible topic. Bev put it well when he heard the message, "I invite you to proceed a little further in fathoming my love, but there is so much more!"

Still, the reality of God's love is an excellent vision as we begin a new millennium. What a strong foundation on which to base our faith and hope!

We are on a voyage of discovery. Each moment presents us with indications of the divine presence. May we always be in search of the love of God in our daily life, always on pilgrimage. What better way to end this book than with a poem by Walt Whitman on spiritual journeying.

> Sail forth—steer for the deep waters only.
> Reckless O Soul, exploring, I with thee, and thou
>   with me,
> For we are bound where mariner has not yet
>   dared to go,
> And we will risk the ship, ourselves and all.
> O my brave Soul! O farther, farther sail!
> O daring joy, but safe! are they not all the seas of
>   God!
> O farther, farther, farther sail!

Endnotes

Chapter One

1. Peter Hannan, S.J., *Nine Faces of God* (Dublin, Ireland: The Columba Press, 1992), p. 11.

2. Ibid.

3. Ibid., p. 15.

4. Max Oliva, S.J., *The Masculine Spirit: Resources for Reflective Living* (Notre Dame, IN: Ave Maria Press, 1997). See Chapter Six for a fuller development of this theme in my life.

5. Rabindranath Tagore, *Gitanjali* (New York: Macmillan Publishing Co., 1913), p. 23. There are many contemporary editions of Tagore's work.

6. David Fleming, S.J., *The Spiritual Exercises of St. Ignatius: A Literal Translation and a Contemporary Reading* (St. Louis: The Institute of Jesuit Sources, 1978), p. 15.

7. Bishop Robert F. Morneau, "The Holy Spirit: Gift to the Church," *Millennium Monthly* (St. Anthony Messenger Press, April 1998).

8. Joseph F. Conwell, S.J., *Impelling Spirit: Revisiting a Founding Experience: 1539 Ignatius Loyola and His Companions* (Chicago: Loyola Press, 1997).

9. Carl Jung, *Man and His Symbols* (New York: Dell Publishing Co., 1971), p. 16.

10. *Julian of Norwich: Showings* (Mahwah, NJ: Paulist Press, The Classics of Western Spirituality Series, 1978), p. 293-295. Also see *Woman: Image of the Holy Spirit* by Joan Schaupp (Dimension Books, 1975).

11. Shirley Du Boulay, "Father Bede's Breakthrough," *The Tablet* (12 September 1998), p. 1180.

12. Ibid.

Chapter Two

1. By Margaret Halaska, O.S.F., unpublished.

2. Roland J. Faley, *Footprints on the Mountain: Preaching and Teaching the Sunday Readings* (Mahwah, NJ: Paulist Press, 1994), p. 609.

3. From *Studies in the Spirituality of Jesuits* (The Seminar on Jesuit Spirituality, May 1998), p. 51. The issue is on Jesuit poetry that reflects the Spiritual Exercises of St. Ignatius of Loyola. The journal is available from: Seminar on Jesuit Spirituality, 3700 West Pine Blvd., St. Louis, MO 63108.

4. Eamon Tobin, *How to Forgive Yourself and Others: Steps to Reconciliation* (Liguori, MO: Liguori Publications, 1993), p. 44.

5. Ibid.

6. Ibid., pp. 46-48.

7. Lewis B. Smedes, *Forgive and Forget: Healing the Hurts We Don't Deserve* (New York: Simon and Schuster, Pocket Books, 1984), p. 102. This is an excellent book, rich in wisdom and practical suggestions for healing.

8. Ibid., p. 104.

9. Ibid., p. 101. See also Margaret Holmgren's article, "Should We Forgive Ourselves?" *The World of Forgiveness*, pp. 12-15. (This is a valuable periodical, published by the International Forgiveness Institute, Madison, WI)

10. John Powell, S.J., *Unconditional Love: Love Without Limits* (Allen, TX: Tabor Publishing, 1978), p. 71.

11. The best treatment of the life of David and its connection to our journey today that I have read is from the book *Leap Over a Wall: Reflections on the Life of David* by Eugene H. Peterson (San Francisco: Harper Collins Paperback, 1998).

12. Eddie Ensley, *Prayer That Heals Our Emotions* (New York: Harper and Row, 1988), pp. 87-88. I have changed this meditation slightly for use on retreats and parish missions.

Chapter Three

1. Jean Pierre de Caussade, S.J., *Abandonment to Divine Providence* (St. Louis, MO: B. Herder Book Company, 1921), p. 15. This is the original text which includes a number of letters, called "Spiritual Counsels," written to Sisters. There is also a modern paperback edition that does not have the letters.

2. Leonard S. Kravitz, "A Martyr for Love," *The Living Pulpit* (July-September 1992), p. 18.

3. de Caussade, S.J., p. 15.

4. James Redfield, *The Celestine Prophecy* (New York: Warner Books, Inc., 1993), pp. 6-7.

5. Jean Pierre de Caussade, *The Joy of Full Surrender* (Orleans, MA: Paraclete Press, 1986), p. 157.

6. Ibid., p. 156.

7. Sister Therese Monaghan is Director of Pastoral Care at St. Vincent's Medical Center in Staten Island, New York.

8. Anne Bryan Smollin, C.S.J., *Tickle Your Soul: Live Well, Love Much, Laugh Often* (Notre Dame, IN: Sorin Books, 1999), pp. 9-10.

9. Ed McGaa, Eagle Man, *Mother Earth Spirituality: Native American Paths to Healing Ourselves and Our World* (San Francisco: Harper Collins Publishers, 1990), pp. 171-172.

10. Sun Bear, Wabun Wind, and Shawnodese, *Dreaming With the Wheel: How to Interpret and Work With Your Dreams Using the Medicine Wheel* (New York: Fireside, 1994), pp. 176 and 268.

11. David Fleming, S.J., *The Spiritual Exercises of St. Ignatius*, p. 141, No. 234 of the Spiritual Exercises.

Chapter Four

1. "The Galilee Song" is from the audio cassette, "Everything I Possess." It is available from Chevalier Music, 51 Mailey St., West Sunshine 3020, Australia. Send $14 U.S. in cash, no checks. The tape is not available in the U.S. or Canada.

2. Two excellent resources on true self-false self are: *New Seeds of Contemplation by Thomas Merton* (New York: A New Directions Book, 1961) and *Merton's Palace of Nowhere: A Search for God Through Awareness of the True Self* by James Finley (Notre Dame, IN: Ave Maria Press, 1978).

3. Michael Cavanagh, *Make Your Tomorrow Better* (Mahwah, NJ: Paulist Press), chapter three.

4. Isaias Powers, C.P., *Quiet Places With Mary: 37 "Guided Imagery" Meditations* (Mystic, CT: Twenty-Third Publications, 1991), pp. 6-7.

Chapter Five

1. Barbara Leahy Shlemon, *Healing Prayer* (Notre Dame, IN: Ave Maria Press, 1976), pp. 13-16.

2. Donald Senior, C.P., "Jesus the Physician: What the Gospels Say About Healing," *Catholic Update* (December 1990).

3. The best treatment of "coming out" issues that I have read is *Loving Someone Gay* by Don Clark, Ph.D. (New York: A Signet Book, New American Library, 1977). It is an excellent resource for anyone interested in being freed from an irrational fear of homosexual people and the various stereotypes many of us have grown up with.

4. Hannan, pp. 29-30.

5. Edward Ingebretsen, S.J., "Diving Into the Wreck," *Studies in the Spirituality of Jesuits* (May 1998), p. 34.

6. Beatrice Bruteau, *The Easter Mysteries* (New York: A Crossroad Book, 1995), pp. 152-153.

7. Daniel Berrigan, S.J., "Show Me Your Face O God" (Psalm 61), *Studies in the Spirituality of Jesuits* (May 1998), p. 22.

8. Dorothy Day was cofounder of the Catholic Worker Movement in the United States, which is both concerned with the basic needs of people trapped in poverty and an end to violence in any form; Cesar Chavez founded the National Farm Worker Movement that gave bargaining rights to farm workers for the first time; Edwina Gateley is a Catholic lay missionary who works with prostitutes in Chicago; Jean Vanier, a Canadian, is the founder of the L'Arche community for people with mental handicaps, which started in France and now has over one hundred communities worldwide.

9. Carlo Maria Martini, S.J., *Perseverance in Trials: Reflections on Job* (Collegeville, MN: The Liturgical Press, 1992), pp. 29-30.

10. "Love Has a Thousand Faces, a Thousand Flavors," an interview with Father Gregory Tolaas by Dawn Gibeau, *Praying* (July 15, 1998), pp. 24-28.

11. Eugene H. Peterson, *Leap Over a Wall: Reflections on the Life of David* (San Francisco: Harper Collins, 1997), chapter seven, "Wilderness."

Chapter Six

1. This chapter was originally published as "A Jesuit's Vision Quest," *Human Development* (Fall, 1997), pp. 19-23. It has been slightly adapted for this book.

2. Barry Lopez, *Crow and Weasel* (New York: Harper Perennial, 1990).

3. Robert A. Johnson, *Inner Work: Using Dreams and Active Imagination for Personal Growth* (HarperSan Francisco: 1986).

4. Ibid.

Chapter Seven

1. Arthur Versluis, *Native American Traditions* (Rockport, ME: Element Books, 1994), p. 34.

2. Two excellent resources for coping with inner desert experiences are: *Along Your Desert Journey* by Robert Hamma (Mahwah, NJ: Paulist Press, 1996) and *Leap Over a Wall: Reflections on the Life of David* by Eugene H. Peterson (San Francisco: Harper Collins, 1997); especially see chapter seven, "Wilderness."

3. For a fuller description of this experience, see my article, "Facing Our Fears in the Call to Act Justly," *Spirituality Today* (Fall, 1985, Vol. 37, no. 3).

4. Rabindranath Tagore, *Gitanjali* (New York: Macmillan, 1913), XXXVII, p. 21.

5. "Isaiah 49" by Carey Landry, North American Liturgy Resources, 1975. Text based on Isaiah 49:15.

6. "She Said Yes: The Unlikely Martyrdom of Cassie Bernall," A Book Review, *The Word Among Us* (November, 1999), pp. 60-63.

7. Misty Bernall, *She Said Yes: The Unlikely Martyrdom of Cassie Bernall;* (Farmington, PA: Plough Publishing House, 1999; 1-800-521-8011). Quotes are from pp. 80-81, 84, 139-140.

8. "Living With Christ" (Novalis, Quebec, Canada; available in United States, 348 RT 11, Champlain, NY 12919), November 1999 issue, p. 143.

9. Victor M. Parachin, "Growing Through Darkness" (Source Unknown; Victor Parachin lives in Claremont, California). In the article, the author adds

a seventh reason to thank God for the dark times in our lives: in the darkness we become less judgmental. Troubles, trials, and tragedies reveal our vulnerability and weakness. These strip us of arrogance, making us less judgmental of others. We become more accepting, understanding and kind after we have been through a fiery trial.

10. Jessica Powers, "The Garments of God," from *Selected Poetry of Jessica Powers* (Kansas City, MO: Sheed and Ward, 1989).

11. Philip C. Blake, S.J., "Learning to Value the Journey," *Human Development* (Volume Six, Number Two, Summer 1985), p. 29, emphasis added.

12. Ibid., p. 30.

Chapter Eight

1. Hannan, p. 105.

2. Found in John Kirvan, *God Hunger: Discovering the Mystic in All of Us* (Notre Dame, IN: Sorin Books, 1999), p. 74.

3. In his insightful book *Mother Earth Spirituality* (San Francisco: Harper Books, 1990), Ed McGaa, Eagle Man, explains the significance of the number four: "There are four faces, or four ages: the face of the child, the face of the adolescent, the face of the adult, the face of the aged. There are four directions or four winds, four seasons, four quarters of the universe, four races of man and woman—red, yellow, black, and white. There are four things that breathe: those that crawl, those that fly, those that are two-legged, those that are four-legged. There are four things above the earth: sun, moon, stars, planets. There are four parts to the green things: roots, stem, leaves, fruit. There are four divisions of time: day, night, moon, year. There are four elements: fire, water, air, earth. Even the human heart is divided into four compartments" (page 33).

4. Long Standing Bear Chief, *Ni-Kso-Ko-Wa: Blackfoot Spirituality, Traditions, Values, and Beliefs* (Browning, MT: Spirit Talk Press, 1992), p. 48. The author is a college professor, artist, aboriginal storyteller, and lecturer. This book is an excellent summary of the aboriginal way of life, past and present.

5. Ibid., p. 39.

6. "How Great Thou Art," written by Stuart K. Hine, Manna Music, Inc., 1953.

7. *How Can I Find God? The Famous and the Not-So-Famous Consider the Quintessential Question,* ed. by James Martin (Liguori, MO: Triumph Books, 1997), p. 156.

8. Taken from *Company,* a magazine of the American Jesuits, Winter 1999/2000, p. 5.

9. From *Christopher News Notes,* No. 336. Address: 12 E. 48th St., New York, NY 10017.

10. *The Calgary Herald,* March 5, 2000.

11. Source unknown.

12. Edouard Glotin, S.J., *Sign of Salvation: The Sacred Heart of Jesus* (Apostleship of Prayer, 3 Stephen Avenue, New Hyde Park, NY 11040), 1989, p. 24.

Chapter Nine

1. The Examen, as it is generally referred to by Jesuits, is more than an examination of conscience. It is a practice that helps us find God more clearly in our daily life. For a fuller explanation, see my book *The Masculine Spirit* (Notre Dame, IN: Ave Maria Press, 1997), pp. 135-140.

2. Joseph A. Tetlow, S.J., "The Most Postmodern Prayer," *Studies in the Spirituality of Jesuits* (January, 1994), pp. 36-37. *Studies* is available from The Seminar on Jesuit Spirituality, 3700 West Pine Blvd., St. Louis, MO 63108.

3. John L. McKenzie, "Aspects of Old Testament Thought," *The Jerome Biblical Commentary* (Englewood, NJ: Prentice-Hall, Inc., 1968) #168, p. 765.

4. Ibid., pp. 765-66.

5. See *Catechism of the Catholic Church*, Numbers 1402-1418.

6. Henri Nouwen, *Our Greatest Gift: A Meditation on Dying and Caring* (Harper and Row, 1994).

7. From *The Word Among Us: Daily Meditations for Lent 2000* (86 Glenholme Ave., Toronto, Ontario, Canada M6H 3B1), p. 63.

8. Beatrice Bruteau, *The Easter Mysteries* (New York: A Crossroad Book, 1995), pp. 151-152. This is a wonderful book for stimulating new reflections on the paschal mystery.

9. Found in Peter Hannan, S.J., *Nine Faces of God* (Dublin, Ireland: The Columba Press, 1992), p. 186.

10. Jessica Powers, *Selected Poetry of Jessica Powers,* ed. Regina Siegfried and Robert Morneau (Kansas City, MO: Sheed and Ward, 1989; now available from ICS Publications, 2131 Lincoln Rd. N.E., Washington, D.C. 20002), p. 53.

11. Michael D. Guinan, O.F.M., "The New Heavens and the New Earth," *Millennium Monthly* (January 2000), p. 4. This is a publication of St. Anthony Messenger Press.

Max Oliva, *S.J.* is the author
of numerous books on prayer and spiritu-
ality, including *The Masculine Spirit:
Resources for Effective Living.* He has led
retreats throughout the U.S., Canada, and
Ireland. He currently ministers on the
Siksika (Blackfoot) Reserve in Alberta,
Canada.